The
ORCHESTRA
of the
LANGUAGE

The

ORCHESTRA

of the

LANGUAGE

by ERNEST M. ROBSON

New York   London

Thomas Yoseloff

Thomas Yoseloff, *Publisher*
11 East 36th Street
New York 16, N. Y.

Thomas Yoseloff Ltd.
123 New Bond Street
London W. 1, England

THE ORCHESTRA OF THE LANGUAGE
has been prepared with
the editorial assistance of
James T. Kennedy, Jr.

The drawings were made by
Marion M. Robson

Printed in the United States of America
American Book–Stratford Press, Inc., New York

TO THOSE WHO HOLD THE IDEA THAT EXPERIMENTAL
RESEARCH IS THE FOUNDATION
OF THE MODERN ARTS

Acknowledgments

SOME SPECIALISTS IN ACOUSTIC ENGINEERING, SPEECH, LINGUISTICS, musicology, and literature have generously given me technical information and their time, privately. The following acknowledgments, however, commit no person mentioned to any responsibility whatsoever for the validity or falsity of the conceptions advanced in this book.

Paul Mills, a founder of the Barbizon Language School, has edited the standard pronunciations in the word lists of the dictionary.

J. B. Kelley of the Bell Laboratories discussed the conditions that determine our judgments of loudness.

Ralph Potter, Director of Transmission Research of the Bell Laboratories, gave valuable advice on the reliability and the limitations of the dimensional information in the spectographs recorded by visible speech instruments.

Edgar Grisewood, New York University, Physics Department, has been in touch with this work during the last few years and has checked the important mathematical data.

Mr. H. K. Dunn, of the Bell Laboratories, assisted me to check on decibel and power data of whispers, conversational speech, singing, and orchestral music.

Margaret Schlauch, linguist and author, former Professor of

English, New York University, has furnished information on the trends in the field of linguistics that have bearing on phonetic intelligence for the writer.

Rudolph R. A. Schramm, musicologist and author, contributed suggestions on the nature of rhythm and recorded the reactions of his music students to tape recordings of material from this book.

George Hibbit, Columbia University, gave references to his work on the time durations of diphthongs of speech. John Black, Ohio State University, supplied data on the mean durations of spoken phrases.

I am also grateful for critical suggestions, advice, and other help from Warren Bower, Dean of the School of General Education, New York University, and from the writer Gladys Birch.

This work would not have been completed without the personal assistance of Adelaide Barbara Conners and Marion Robson.

Introduction

THIS BOOK IS FOR THE READER WHO ENJOYS LANGUAGE MUSIC. It is also for those who have some technical interest in the phonetic patterns of speech that a writer can intentionally incorporate in the script. The technical aspects of using the latent whispers inherent in written words are presented in the first part of this book. Without the phonetic instruments discussed in the technical presentation, the music which appears in the third section could not possibly have been written.

The creations of a poetry of feeling were and are practical proofs that the sound dimensions of speech can be used to compose as well as to analyze. They were the experimental proving grounds for the phonetic instruments developed in Part I. Nor were they mere technical exercises. They were serious attempts to produce works of linguistic art. Their success is to be judged by their capacity to make words more effectively express emotions and ideas . . . and to suggest new forms of language.

Apart from their aesthetic value, these procedures have been used commercially. One of the leading advertising copywriters has applied them for the refinement of his writing. The principles in this book are being used by Mr. Paul Mills and Mr. Bernard Roberts to teach the sales personnel of large corporations how to use speech more effectively.

The phonetic data, concepts, and procedures are organized as a writer's manual on the sound dimensions of speech. Historically, this may be the first time that those properties and relationships of the sounds of speech that specifically apply to writing have been schematically presented. Although all the information in Part I can be summed up in one page of reference tables in Part II, the development of the concepts that guided the experiments and the selection of data are explained throughout Part I in ten chapters of illustrated excerpts from famous passages of writing. Naturally, the explanatory section may have value for teachers of writing as well as for professional writers.

If the reader has no technical interests, he should skip Parts I and II and enjoy the twenty-two lyrics that constitute the last section of this book. They are language compositions. These, like any other new music, need some extra listening. A first reading aloud of the compositions, then one silently, then a second reading aloud, will give the writing a fair chance to be heard and understood.

Three poets influenced this book: Walt Whitman, Edgar Allan Poe, and Hart Crane.

The fact that a theme or subject matter can determine a literary style came to me from Walt Whitman. His *Leaves of Grass* is an illustration of a loose, rolling, redundant style being literally forced into existence by the writer's need for more freedom to express the expanding spaces, the growing massiveness, and the proliferating multitudes of an independent people sensing its continental destiny and its incipient world power.

It was Poe who considered the physical properties of words as elements out of which he could consciously construct a language composition. He clarified the problem of intentionally designing a poem to express specific emotions and act as a machine to induce an effect in the mind of an audience. This made a poet the engineer of literary effects. Poe proved that the aesthetic power of language depended to a considerable degree on the sounds of words. And he broadened, critically, the verbal art of selecting visual images as representations of feeling that could convert emotional associations into affective symbols. In the field of experimental poetry an object of this book is to carry on the project that Poe began.

Hart Crane learned how the sounds of words could bombard his mind and evoke feelings out of associations dormant in his subconscious. Some of the images in the compositions of Part III were developed out of this technique. But they are always used as elements in the larger-sound-image of a composition.

Each lyric in this book is an answer to one of two questions:

1. To what theme or subject does this or that phase of phonetic writing lend itself most effectively? What will it most fittingly *describe* and *demonstrate?* The basic concept here put forward is that literary art (to the extent that it is an art) is a *demonstrative description* with sound images. This approach uses the language medium as the subject and starting point. Then it seeks the most suitable nonlinguistic theme.

2. The second approach is the more obvious one. The theme or subject is first established. Then the question arises: what phonetic instrument is most appropriate to express the subject?

Because different themes require different phonetic techniques, no two compositions are written in exactly the same style.

The thematic materials are nature, animals, and musical instruments. The outlook on nature is not sentimental. It is colored by some training as a chemist. Nor are animal themes enveloped with the effeminate sentiments usually associated with poetry. The writer was an animal trapper.

One other concept might be of interest. That is the idea of building a bridge or a connecting link between the mental orientations of the engineer and the artist. A quantitative treatment of the physical elements of speech as so many variables and the construction of standard curves from these variables to reveal meaning are parts of the mental behavior of the scientist or engineer. On the other hand, the use of these curves as emotionally charged sound images is decidedly not scientific. It is the behavior of the artist who creates a composition of feeling with subjective symbols.

Both orientations are implicit in the style of the lyrics. In that sense, the style itself is symbolic because it incorporates values it was designed to express.

Contents

Part I

Written Acoustic Patterns:
The Sound Dimensions of the Writer's Art

1

Basic Considerations

THE PAINTER HAS HIS COLORS, THE COMPOSER HIS NOTES AND instruments, but what are the materials, the physical tools of the writer?

This book is one answer to this question.

Furthermore, this question implies a basic idea that underlies this research. It is: the physical properties of every art medium create the descriptive, semantic, and imaginative potentials of the producer as an artist. It does not follow that all significant writing must be good art, and vice versa. But the assumption was made, and is held, that every outstanding aesthetic achievement and part of the effectiveness of the communicative process itself depend on the physical properties of the signals that constitute the medium—here the language medium.

This book concentrates on the auditory signals that a writer can incorporate in the script.

Auditory signals have a special service to contribute to the writer, because of the subjective themes of the literary imagination. They impinge on the auras of infancy and the memories of childhood; and they can express, uniquely, a language of feeling.

Every child is taught to read by identifying the sounds of

speech or the phonetic units of words with the written hiero-
glyphs of the alphabet. Childhood conditioning here, as in other
behavior, runs through the reading habits of the adult. That is
why reading is always an oral memory and an unconscious
vocalization of speech. Because words carry speech and hearing
that began in infancy and voice recollections that date from the
reading days of childhood, their phonetic patterns are associated
with our most sustained emotions and feelings. Auditory images
are far more entwined with our emotional roots than the logical
abstract or the later graphic image carried by words.

When we analyze any process thoroughly at least three approaches must be applied: the physical factors, the structure,
and the purpose of the process. Here the physical factors are the
tone, timbre, time, and power of the speech that a writer can
incorporate in the script. The structure is the pattern characteristics of these factors. The purpose is to sharpen the power of
words and to make the writer's language more effective.

Since we are dealing with the ear values in the words of
written speech, these techniques may be concisely summarized
as "audio-scriptics." By definition, "audio-scriptics" are *the techniques for the writer to make written language more effective
with patterns of the tone, timbre, time, and power in the sounds
of speech.*

The phonetic variables tone, time, and power have been calibrated to communicate with a *probable* reader or listener. That
is the writer's public. Therefore, the time values of phonemes
and words are standardized to eliminate an uncontrollable number of minute differences in the speeds of speech. They are
average durations in centiseconds. They can be speeded up or
slowed down for different rates of speech. Accordingly, these
are the time values a writer can use. When we listen to the
durations of the words in the phrase: "A strange man," obviously
the word "A" is the shortest, "man" is next in duration, and
"strange" is clearly the word with the longest extension in time.

There is no question that a speaker or a singer can stretch out the time duration of a short word, or contract the duration of a long word. What is meant here by the time extension of words is their *natural tendency* to consume speaking time at a normal rate of speech, i.e., about 150 words per minute. But these natural tendencies exist. Since the writer does not interpret speech as an announcer, or actor, or a director, the vocal tendencies of words are the only tools he possesses to endow his script with the potential of effective language for a reader or a speaker.

The same considerations have been given to the tone and power variables. Their numbers indicate only the *relative average levels* of the tones and powers of syllables or words. Hence they offer the writer an opportunity to produce sound images that will communicate to others. If he sets up the peculiar traits in his own voice as a standard, then he talks only to himself.

Here we face the dividing line between establishing written language and interpreting it with speech. The difference is between composition and performance. The golden overtones in F.D.R.'s radio voice were priceless assets, as is the rasping guttural idiom of Jimmy Durante. But these qualities appear in the renditions of a script, not in it. A writer who has something to say, and wishes to express his subject matter with effective sound images, cannot base his auditory intelligence entirely on any bias of the voice. Some standardization (as in musical notation) is the price that must be paid by the writer who wishes to create images that will be intelligible to more than a handful of aesthetes.

The auditory is one of several forms of literary intelligence. Words may be used to refer to ocular perceptions and to arrange images in rhythmic patterns. "The white sun of the mackerel sky," "The triangles were in the shadows of the buildings," "The buck's antlers triggered the stars" are graphic images. They are the work of the mind's eye. Authors with vivid visual imagina-

tions concentrate on imagistic writing. Words may also pointedly
refer to actions stripped of all sensory characteristics. These are
events such as "Joe hit Bill," "When a vacuum increases the
temperature falls," etc. This use of language relies on the mind's
reason. It may operate quite formally as in such logical statements as: "Prime numbers, such as 19 and 23, are divisible only
by 1 or by themselves," "To be or not to be, that is the question."

The distinctions just made are necessarily analytical. The craft
of writing depends on continuous co-ordinations of the mind's
eye, the mind's ear, and the mind's reason. These three mental
processes are interrelated and interdependent. Audio-scriptic intelligence, the creation of the mind's ear, is therefore intimately
involved with all the functions of the literary imagination, and
has bearing on all the basic questions that arise in the art of
writing.

There are certain requirements for applying these techniques
with phonetic intelligence. One is to hear, accurately hear, the
tones, powers, time-periods, and timbres of speech. It may seem
obvious to say that audio-scriptic skill cannot even begin to
develop until the writer hears with discrimination the latent
speech in words. Yet many writers (like many other people) are
practically deaf to the tones of speech and to the finer differences in intensity among syllables. One of the contributions of
this procedure is to train the ear of the writer to hear what he
is talking about. Another requirement for applying these methods is to learn how to graph syllables so that their time, tone,
and power patterns may be drawn on paper with clear contours
that fix sounds in the reader's memory and extend his audio-
visual imagination.

Most writers will agree that rhythm in writing is important for
fashioning style, for the articulations of thought and feeling, and
for general freedom of expression. But most writers fail to realize
that the rhythms of their words depend on shifts in the time

durations of conversational speech. Time is a most decisive dimension of language, because the stop and flow of thought measurably changes with a stop and flow of time. Conversation runs on in time continuously and adjusts the durations of its outbursts and pauses to the requirements of breathing, the emphases of meaning, and the speed of hearing. Time durations of the reader's attention span make the length of sentences a factor in the readability of prose.

An early stage in developing audio-scriptic intelligence is the perception of the time value of syllables, words, phrases, pauses, and paragraphs. A later stage is to see the rises and the falls in the tones of words and the powers of words that move with the passage of time. The final stage of phonetic control is to create or analyze language from the point of view of a word composer, a point of view not too different from that of a musical composer. This is the stage where leadership can arise. The patterns of speech may organize tone to make writing sing. They can use timbre to make statements decisive. They can feature time and power values to make the writer's ideas and thoughts rhythmic and clear. The full orchestration of our voice in written language, as the full instrumental score of a musical orchestra, offers this creative opportunity. The writer may create new sound-images that will develop new hearing habits and new auditory feelings and emotions in a new audience. This is the writer's ideal audience—in distinction to his probable one.

The explanation of audio-scriptic intelligence is based on answers to two questions, one of which considers psychological conditions, the other acoustic factors. What gives to sound images their descriptive, associative, and expressive powers? What are the acoustic facts that underlie the effectiveness of words when arranged into configurations of sound?

The effectiveness of phonetic patterns depends on this psychological principle. Any structure or pattern of our recorded sense impressions is capable of describing a theme or subject matter whose elements have a similar structure. These recorded configurations of our senses help us to find our way around in the world of emotions more precisely, and to achieve a fuller mental orientation. They act as sensory maps. Therefore, when a rhythm of the tone or power of speech sounds possesses a pattern similar to the rhythm of a moving object, or a feeling, or a developing situation, then the acoustic pattern has descriptive value. Rhythms or patterns of the percussive, hissing, humming, and other timbres of the voice may punctuate with breaks, stops, and changing speeds the breaks, stops, slowdowns, and quickenings of thought and feeling. This, too, is a descriptive power.

Obviously, a sharpening of our sensory perception increases our descriptive powers. A phonetically controlled script does this in four ways:

It separates the tones from the noises of speech. This isolation creates the foundation for building sound images with words.

It fixes auditory perception by graphic images on paper. This aids memory.

It reveals the ideal nature of speech sounds from a writer's viewpoint. These are the clearest sounds, the ones the writer wishes the reader to hear with the greatest degree of certainty.

It gives the writer additional time to listen to the auditory patterns in his language and to develop hearing habits of a critical and creative character.

A minimal service of these techniques is this indisputable fact: they unscramble some of the uncertainties and the slurs in conversational speech, and the hearing of it.

Syllables are composites of vowels that are tones, consonants that are noises, and semivowels or transient tones. When we pronounce the syllables and words of natural speech, their tones and intensities continuously pass into one another, and blend, scramble, and blur. Boundaries between syllables and words are not clear-cut. They over-lap. It is the nature of the human voice to change slightly the tones of vowels in the neighborhood of different consonants. The sounds of speech are smudged by these indefinite articulations. Effort is necessary for precise articulation. No one wants to do unnecessary work. Therefore, the energy level of speech is usually dropped down and its contours weakened to the minimum requirement for communication. Although there is a security margin of loudness, it is small.

The longer we hear a tone, the clearer it becomes. Speech rates that vary between 175 and 225 words per minute do not give the ear much time to discriminate pure tones. The minimum period of time for the ear to catch any tone value whatsoever lies between 0.02 and 0.03 seconds. Several of the short, speedy vowels do not last longer than 0.04 to 0.05 seconds, even at moderate rates of speech.

The high speeds and muddled articulations of normal speech interfere with discriminations of tones from intensities of diction. The effect on hearing can be compared with a stroboscopic color (Fig. 1). Imagine the white spokes of a wheel as the vowel tones, the black spokes as consonantal noises. When the wheel rapidly rotates, the impression on the ear is gray.

Figure 1

Clear discrimination of tones and intensities of speech.

Blurring of tones and intensities of speech.

Audio-scriptic intelligence slows down the spinning of the wheel. It extends the time for hearing speech, isolates and breaks down the tones and noises of vowels and consonants, and suggests how patterns of these acoustic elements, i.e., sound images, may add another dimension to verbal communication.

The purpose of this book is to make this type of intelligence more available to the writer. In effect, here are new literary instruments. The most novel tools for the writer in this book are the phonetic tables in Part II, which for the first time give the writer an opportunity to build up a vocabulary based exclusively on the sounds of words. These tables will assist the writer to coin new words, nonsense syllables, phrases, and longer idioms of expression. They will help the writer to estimate the time, tone, and power of words. Accompanying these tables are instructions for their proper use. The fact that all the information in this book is summed up in Table 1 of Part II is a simplification that will save time in giving phonetic values to words.

The practical services of these techniques for sharpening the auditory intelligence and the effectiveness of writing have been discussed. Another broader implication should be considered. Any increase of our descriptive powers is an extension of consciousness. A new sentience awakens in some persons a new interest in processes that they wish to describe and communicate to others. It is no accident that men's imaginations have invariably been captured by any technique that lets them experiment with new forms of expression to refine and acquire more control of their minds. They do sense that new powers to illuminate experience do retroactively lead them on to more worlds of experience in the light of new perspectives. The expansion of music is inconceivable without the development of notational techniques. Progress in mathematics preceded many of the most important advances in physics. It is difficult to consider the linguistic and poetic contributions of the Elizabethan drama without the blank verse it inherited, or the structural austerity of the classic French stage without the Alexandrian couplet, or western European literature during the last hundred years without the symbolist technique that Poe developed in his *Philosophy of Composition* and in his essay, "How I Wrote 'The Raven.'"

2

Historical Perspective

THE HISTORY OF PHONETIC INTELLIGENCE SHOWS THAT ALL GOOD writers have used it unintentionally and intentionally in varying degrees.

Rime, centuries ago, was associated with reason. It is a device for controlling rhythms by stabilizing the tone of a vowel with a consonant. A fixed consonant holds the overtone pattern of the vowel. This artifice, when repeated, overcomes the uncertainties in our hearing of the muddled, indefinite tones in speech. Edgar Allen Poe consciously used vowel rhythms to stylize his prose. He did the same thing for his poetry. The rime pattern of the sonnet originated to punctuate a single thought or emotion. Dante converted a triple end-rime scheme into a symbol of the Holy Trinity. The rhythms of free verse depend on the habit of American and English speech to extend the time duration and to increase the audibility of a syllable at the end of a phrase or sentence. This technique has been converted into a radio style by Frank Brookhauser, the leading commentator of Philadelphia. He orally punctuates his thoughts by extending the time duration of the last word in every sentence.

About 1870, the French poet, Arthur Rimbeau, saw a new

importance in the use of vowels. Specific vowels, he claimed, could be identified with definite colors. He associated the colder colors, blue and green, with the more voluminous back vowels *oo* as in *moon* and *oh* in *old*, and the color red with the high, front vowel *ee*. When the tour through Rockefeller Center halts among the solemn shadows under the dark marble columns of the huge lounge of Radio City Music Hall, the voices of the crowd become low and subdued. The guide of the tour announces that visitors to this large, dark room always talk in hushed and lowered tones. The Public Relations Department of Radio City Music Hall verifies this observation on the basis of reports on thousands of tours. We see here a tendency for the energy and oral shapes of speech to be influenced by a feeling for the quality of our physical surroundings. We modify our speech to express the feeling. At Ohio University Professor J. W. Black carefully tested the speaking rate and the intensity of the voices of students reading aloud short phrases in rooms of different sizes, shapes, and reflection powers. His instrumental measurements showed that in larger rooms the time duration of speech is unquestionably prolonged and there is a tendency for the voice to lower its decibel level.

In 1939 the linguistic scholar, E. Prokosch, noticed that persons without musical or phonetic training interpreted certain vowels as "low," others as "high." He illustrated this with child talk in the nursery. "A little steam engine tries to climb a hill and says cheerfully, 'I think I can, I think I can.' But the hill is too steep; the poor little engine slides back and says sadly, 'I thought I could, I thought I could.'" The vowels in "I think I can" are the front vowels and express with greater tension in the vocal chords a high and intense feeling for success and action going on in the present. "I thought I could" is composed of "low" vowels and expresses melancholy in retrospective memory. Other experimenters in "phonetic symbolism" have made statistical studies that show a definite trend for the back vowels to be associated with concepts of largeness and darkness, the tight front vowels with the tiny and the bright.

When Dizzy Dean announced, "He slud into third," he intuitively voiced more phonetic intelligence with the word *slud* than he would have expressed with the word *slid*. The St. Louis English teachers who publicly protested against Dean's language were evidently ignorant of the fact that *slud* more aptly describes a low, dirt-thudding slide than *slid* with its high, weak little vowel. Actually, Dean was unconsciously creating a portmanteau word, like "brunch" out of breakfast and lunch. *Slud* condenses *thud* and *slide*. The low, powerful vowel in *slud* is most appropriate.

Gertrude Stein repeated phrases and sentences in blocks, and arranged her reiterations in time with rhythmic value for representing feelings as though she were a musical composer.

Billy Rose, after much research work on the vowels used in the best sellers among popular songs, discovered the melodic appeal of the low and middle vowels: *oo* and *ah*. He then wrote "Barney Google With the Goo-Goo Googly Eyes." The Barney Google cartoon was his gimmick. This concocted piece of tin-pan phoneticism made money in spite of being characterized by Deems Taylor as "probably the worst song in the history of the music business." It may be an understatement to suggest that this is a limited application of audio-scriptic intelligence.

The acoustician and psychologist, Richard Paget, interpreted the moving shapes of the chambers in the mouth as phonetic gestures. To him, the tongue, teeth, lips, and cheeks behaved almost like actors in a little oral theater. Their dramatic pantomimes were compared to gestures and were considered the foundations of meaning and originators of the roots of words in all languages. James Joyce was familiar with this theory of Paget. He used linguistic gestures in his multilingual, audio-scriptic epic, *Finnegan's Wake*.

The Visible Speech program of the Bell Laboratories developed a symbolic language on the basis of the overtone patterns of vowels and semivowels and the tone levels of consonants marked by their effect on neighboring vowels. This is a language of spectographic symbols that records and objectively represents the real tone elements of speech. The symbolism is simpler and far more significant, acoustically, than the symbols of other so-called universal or international alphabets. It shows the relative time durations as well as details on the overtones of speech and has considerably more information to contribute to the writer's understanding of phonetic dimensions than other phonetic alphabets.

The arithmetic values for the time, tone, and power of the elements of speech presented in the tables of Part II and used in the phonetic analyses of this book were based on studies of the measurements of reliable acoustic laboratories and on the findings of speech specialists in several universities. They were then tested out in the process of writing and subjected to tests from the point of view of their practical value for the writer.

3

The Orchestra of the Language

TIMBRE IS THE SPECIAL AND DISTINCTIVE QUALITY OF A SOUND.
If a musician hears a bass violin, a bassoon, and a tuba play
the same note with the same loudness, he can detect which instrument is making the note. That is what timbre means to a
musician. He may call it musical "color." Our sensing of timbre
need not be restricted to musical instruments. If differences in
pitch and loudness are disregarded, then any sound that enables
a person to identify and distinguish the nature of its source
possesses a recognizable quality. That quality is timbre.

The quality of sound has been attacked as a special problem
by research scientists. It is not a simple one. The acoustic elements of timbres are the pattern or structure of their overtones,
the speed with which they build up their tones and intensities,
and the speed with which they die down or decay. Large changes
in intensity and frequency affect quality. While intensity and
frequency are related and modify one another, the effect of
their interactions depends on the dimension of time.

Behind the complex configurations of sound quality lie the
nature and structure of the material at the source of the sound.

Phonetic timbre is the distinctive quality in the sounds of

29

words that enable a writer to sense and to identify the organs of speech that produce them. The timbre of words is the cast of the voice in them. This depends on the structure and the physical traits of the tongue, teeth, lips, palate, vocal chords, and oral liquids that modulate the passage of breath when we talk. The tongue, lips, cheeks, lower jaw, and vocal chords are the moving organs of speech whose motions continually alter the shape of the chambers inside the mouth. The quality of articulation is sharply affected by these changes in the shape of the oral chambers, and by the position and structure of the nasal cavities, the spacing of the teeth, and by the form of the hollows in the throatal or pharyngeal regions. The timbre in the ear values of words also depends on the density and elasticity of the organs of speech. Density and elasticity are two somewhat basic acoustic considerations of all materials at the source of sound. Our identification or recognition of the acoustic face, the memorable phonetic features of words, such as their liquidity, solidity, airiness, pliability, tension, and softness are influenced by the trembling impressions of the density and elasticity of the teeth, tongue, palate, lips, cheeks, vocal chords, and oral saliva upon the pulse of speech. These physical traits stamp their imprint upon our auditory intelligence with a certain decisiveness and finality in the quality of articulation. This auditory quality can be compared to the effect of a conspicuous blend of color upon the eye.

A writer's interest in the timbres of speech is the lift they may give to his creative imagination and their assistance to his craftsmanship. A word technician is concerned with how auditory qualities can express his thoughts, feelings, and emotions with more precise shades of meaning, greater accuracy in description, and a more decisive power of statement. He is not directly interested in all the articulatory gymnastics involved in the physiological explanations of phonetics by speech pedagogues. A writer wants the facts about phonetic timbre simplified so he can use them. The first step in this direction is to reduce the complexities of articulation qualities to a number of auditory impressions or casts of the voice upon hearing as though they were a set of physiological colors. From this viewpoint, the writer's point of view, the timbres of language are the *audible* casts of the voice in words such as: the boniness or hardness of the consonant *k* (carries a bony roof-of-the-mouth color); the liquid soft bubbliness of *b* (stamped with the interior moisture of bulbous-shaped lips); the harsh raucousness and the oral roar of the vocal chords and the throatal resonance of *r*; the almost pure, breathlike airiness of *h*; and the minute sharpness in the dental detonation of *t*. Further simplification of these casts of the voice in words is to classify them as phonetic instruments in a complete orchestra of the language whose intelligent use depends on the direction of the writer.

Please turn to Figure 2. Here the sounds of speech have been arranged in the image of a 41-piece orchestra waiting to be organized by the auditory imagination of the writer, the director, and the composer of language.

The illustration shows vowels, diphthongs, semivowels, and consonants arranged in eleven orchestral groups. These musical images will help the writer or speaker to visualize the letters of the alphabet as symbols of timbre and instruments of phonetic intelligence. Just as a symphonic orchestra puts the stringed instruments and the wood winds in the front rows and the percussion devices such as drums, triangles, cymbals back in the rear rows, so the orchestra of the language places the vowels that are tones in the front and the consonants that are noises in the back. Although this arrangement grew out of an analogy with music, it is based on the valid acoustic distinction between a tone and a noise. This auditory distinction leads the writer to look at the alphabet as he must look at it if he intends to use the timbres of speech to develop audio-scriptic intelligence.

The first three groups are tone divisions. They separate the

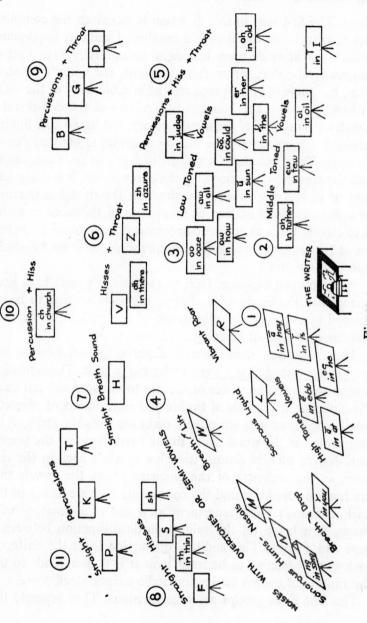

THE ORCHESTRA OF THE LANGUAGE

Figure 2

vowels into three tone levels: high, middle, and low. Since the vowels are the most potent creators of tone in language, this scheme prepares the writer to think about vowels and to hear their vibrations as notes in a vowel scale. Later, the vowel scale and its uses in writing will be discussed in detail. At present, the writer should keep one fact in mind. These "tones" are produced in the mouth, not in the throat or the vocal chords. The "high" vowels ee, ĕ, ĭ, etc., are made in the front one of the two chambers that the tongue makes by separating the hollow of the mouth into two resonating rooms. The tongue acts like a wall. The "low" tone vowels such as oo, oh, aw are produced by drawing back and dropping the tongue-wall so that the oral chamber is lengthened, deepened, and enlarged. The strongest overtones of the low-toned vowels come from the rear of the mouth, out of whose depths they carry to our hearing a feeling of lowness, largeness, and darkness. The "middle" vowels are compromises. This group includes the diphthongs oi and ew that fuse a low and high vowel, and the vowel ah whose oral structure lies midway between the high and low vowels.

Let us look again at the illustrated orchestra.

Behind the full-toned vowels in the first three groups appear the partial tones, the transient semivowels in Group 4: w, y, r, l, m, n, ng. The last three of these sounds, m, n, ng, resonate with vibrations in the nasal cavities that give them a humming quality. The hum of m, lower in tone level than n, is heard most clearly in words with low-toned vowels such as hum, room, strum, mum, mumbles, murmur, mom, momentum. When m borders on a low- or middle-tone vowel, its hum color is more powerful than in the high-vowel environment of words such as maim, member, mammy, mimic, minimize. The higher vowels break up sharply the low throb in m's resonance and mask its hums. This observation suggests a tendency in many semivowels to sound clearer when they blend with vowels on the same tone level. The vowel sustains the altitude of the transient tone. Otherwise, hearing is compelled to make too many adjustments in too short a period of time. We see here how delicate these qualities are and how necessary it is to use all the elements of auditory intelligence in a related pattern to make a definite impression on the ear.

The hum-timbre of *n*, higher in tone than *m*, is more impressive in high-voweled words: *keen, kin, pin, tin-pan, Dane, insane, winnow, wind, stain.* If we listen closely to the humming resonance of *ng* in *bang, cling, dung, wrung, ding-dong, clang, gong, whang, singsong,* the denseness of the nasal quality is noticeable. The peculiar, blurred, dense hums of *ng* are the effect of its closely packed overtones. The dense timbre of *ng* is uninfluenced by the tone levels of neighboring vowels.

There is something of the plasticity, softness, and liquidity of the tongue in the timbre of *l* that tinges words such as *lingual, loll, wallow, swill, lolli* in lollipop. When the low-tone level of *l* precedes a vowel and introduces a word, it conveys a sense of uplift in such expressions as *left, lift, lilt, laugh, lady, light, lick, leap, lip.* But the low-tone level of *l* may have an opposite effect when it follows a vowel or terminates a word. Then it can give the impression of a physical letdown, a leveling off, or a long drop: i.e., *lull, fall, tail, stale, spill, fallow, keel, dull, pall, shawl, kill, cool, sprawl.*

These examples should show the writer that the use of phonetic timbre is a creative opportunity, and not a gadgetlike gimmick of mechanical character. Its value is a potential for the writer's imagination, and not a guarantee.

Three of the more powerful semivowels in Group 4 of the illustrated orchestra are *y, r,* and *w*. The low-toned timbre of open, loose-lipped *w* sweeps its upcurve of breath out of the low chordal regions of resonance, and glides into vowels at high speed, and with force. The power and the tubal openness in the swift upswerve of this sound has creative possibilities for the writer. The timbre of *w* may be used to suggest the open-flowing, the rhythmic, the forceful, or combinations of these qualities. These possibilities are conveyed in *win, wild, water, wings, wobble, waves, wind, wanton, whiff, warble, whistle, swish, swing, sway, willow, wail, will,* and (again with deference to Dizzy Dean), *swang.* The power and the conspicuous quality of *w* can put a definitive pulse into phrases, e.g., *the wishing well, wanton wenches, the Wailing Wall, wishy-washy, winning ways, wild women, werewolf.* The timbre of transient-toned *y,* with its speed and gliding power suddenly emitted from the high tone region in the mouth, strikes the ear with some of the chordal tension of the vowel *ee.* This explosion of high tension may be used to express the assertive, the abrupt, the final, or the swiftly rising impetus in *yield, youth, yank, yell, yip, yap, yes, yeast.* The throatal, low roar of *r,* full of pharyngeal friction, has a resonance that is reinforced by the sympathetic vibration of the tip or blade of the tongue, near the center of the hard palate; *r* carries its low-toned roughness, power, and its dark throat color into low-toned words such as *strong, storm, harsh, war, rough, burr, hard, rock, hoarse, char, gore, gorge, wrong.* The sense of irritation and power displayed in these words is partly due to the chordal friction and the tremendous intensity in the ear-color of *r.* Although *r* is low-toned, its timbre is not destroyed by gliding into high-toned vowels in words such as *leer, rage, rile, liar, cheer, rasp, rant, ram, wretch, bear, rape.* Here its power is evident. Engineering data on the acoustic dimensions of *r* show it to be the most powerful of all nonvowel speech sounds. That is the probable explanation of why the timbre of *r* is not destroyed by running into vowels on quite different tone levels.

The straight percussion sounds that strike the ear like drums appear in the noise section of the orchestra of the language, high up in the last row. They are the breath-exploding consonants *p, k,* and *t.* They do explode. The pentup air pressure suddenly released by the noise of *p* has a lip timbre; *t,* a teeth quality; and *k,* a hard texture that echoes from the bony roof of the mouth. These are the swiftest sounds of speech, whose time durations are so tiny that the ear has little opportunity to detect tone. The timbre of the percussions in orchestral Group 11 is not influenced by the tones of adjacent vowels. The lip explosiveness of p sounds through *nipple, pucker, pop, pout, lip, pulp, flip, pipe.* The sharp, quick, abrupt, dental cast of t carries its keen timbre into *taut, meat, tear, cut, tattle, teeth, white, tart, tight, tack;* and its quality of the diminutive and the swift into *tot, trout, teat, tut-tut, titter.* The boniness of the roof of the mouth enters into the articulation of k and passes its quality of hardness on with speed and sharpness in *crack, truck, cluck, conk, kick, click, knock, creak, squeak, ack-ack, nick.*

If you try to pronounce p, k, t with resonance in the throat, your articulations begin to sound like b, g, d. These resonated plosives constitute orchestral Group 9. Their throatal vibrations lengthen the durations of b, g, d, and this extra time for hearing permits the ear to perceive more tone than in the snappy, unvoiced percussives, p, k, t. The timbre of b is impressed with a sense of the softness of bulbous-shaped lips. It has the quality of a relatively slow explosion moving softly, amorphously, with low tone through a wet bag. Words such as *lob, blimp, bubble, bobble, blab, blubber, sob, babble, boob, slob, burp, bib, bulb, babe* communicate a sense of full-blown moisture, or slowness, or lack of structure, or a combination of these characteristics. The source of g is about five times as far back from the surface of the front teeth as its relative k. The timbre of g is an explosive gutturalness shot through with power, duration, and indefiniteness in tone. When g occurs twice in a word it gives the effect of a guttural noise bouncing up and down like a stammering in the throat in *goggles, gag, groggy, gargle, gig, agog, geegaw.* These words are double acoustic images of the guttural colored emissions of breath that the back of the tongue explodes in the glottal regions. The sudden tongue-dropped, openmouthed throatiness of g casts its timbre like a shadow of the voice upon the expression of words like *gawk, gasp, gook, gape.*

The hissing consonants in orchestral Group 3 have the frictional quality of breath blowing tiny, aerial bubbles over the lips and tongue and through the teeth. They are *th, sh, f,* and *s.* Some of these sounds are long-durational and all of them have a soft texture, except *s,* which carries the sharp imprint of the teeth. Their timbre of fricative breath, beating in the ear like an atomized gas, pulses through words such as *fast, swift, slash, swish, hiss, fizzle, fuss, sift, soufflé, shuffle, scuffle.* The longer time duration of steady breath friction reveals its dimension in *stiff, staff, suffer, shaft, smooth, stuff.* Notice how the soft-lipped, air-rippled quality of *f* enters expressions such as *fluff, ruffle, foam, muff,* and how the carnivorous teeth emotionally color the breath with the sharpness and snap of *s* in *hiss, snip, sizzle, cuss, slash, sik'em.*

These examples can be multiplied to show that the timbre groups in the illustrated orchestra of the language will aid the writer to select more powerful, more sensuous, and phonetically more intelligent words. But the writer might remember this fact. The timbre of consonants and semivowels was usually considered in conjunction with the other dimensions of audio intelligence: time, tone, power. Although timbre is a tool for making language decisive, its impressions on hearing are limited. Sharp contours of timbre depend on all the dimensions of sound to communicate their full meaning. So does audio-scriptic intelligence.

We can draw these conclusions: The greater the number of sound dimensions the writer can control, the greater his potential for creating sound images rich with phonetic information. The greater the concentration of auditory signals throughout a flow of words written to produce a clear auditory effect, the greater the probability that the intended effect will be heard. Concentration is important. The reason for its importance is the weak energy of conversational speech.

The measurable energy region of audio-scriptic intelligence lies between a whisper and loud conversational speech. Decibel measurements at the source of the sound waves reveal that the power in ordinary speech has approximately one hundred times the power of a whisper. This range covers the vocalized auditory impressions or "ear values" of words seen by the eye when reading words on a printed page and applies to most of the dramatic speech we hear from the legitimate stage, radio, video, and motion pictures. See Figure 3.

The energy level of normal conversational speech is the standard for all the calculations of the ear values of words that appear in this book. "Normal" is an approximate 60-decibel level of heard speech. Consideration was given to the auditory impressions of phonemes when whispered and spoken loudly. All the oral memories in our reading originated from the energy levels of conversational speech. When a dramatist or any other writer reads his script aloud to himself, he tries to speak naturally. To do this he must maintain the loudness level of ordinary conversation. One of the miracles of human hearing and speech is our ability to hear the loudness of our own talk approximately as others hear it. These are the considerations for taking the energy level of conversational speech as the standard for estimating audio-scriptic intelligence.

When we speak we slur the sounds; when we read, we skip and slur them. The experienced copywriter knows he cannot write the same way for radio and video as he does for the printed page. So does the playwriter. The rhythms of the words, the pausing and timing of the phrases must be written to be spoken by an actor. The songwriter must choose words that bring out the resonance in the singing voice, that permit the holding of pitch, the timing of notes, the control of breathing, that accent the measures and above all that tell the stories in the dynamic rhythms of the music. These requirements and the problems they pose for the writer are involved with the limited amount of

Comparative powers (in terms of pressure, dynes per cm²) of Conversational Speech, Loud Speech, the Singing Voice, and a 75-piece orchestra. A whisper has roughly $\frac{1}{2000}$ the power of Conversational Speech.

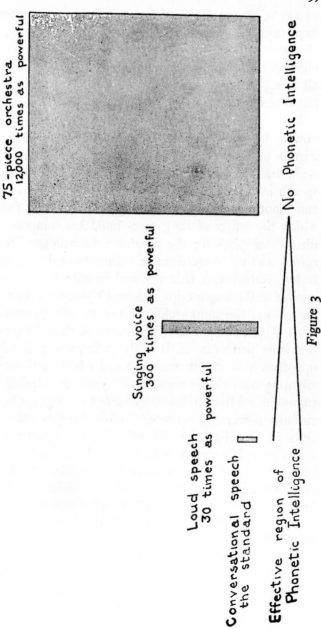

75-piece orchestra
12,000 times as powerful

Singing voice
300 times as powerful

Loud speech
30 times as powerful

Conversational speech
the standard

Effective region of
Phonetic Intelligence

No Phonetic Intelligence

Figure 3

energy in speech. This ever-present energy condition is broadly but concisely presented in Figure 3. In considering this table, the writer should remember that just as the color of flames changes with temperature, so the qualities and properties of all things, sounds included, are radically affected by their inherent energy.

It will be seen, from the point of view of a table of sheer power, how tiny and ineffective conversation appears (see Figure 3) when thrown against the voluminous tones of the orchestra, the chordal pulse of song, or a powerful burst of speech in a staged play. Yet it is the sensitivity, expressiveness, and emotional clarity of the writing that is the foundation on which the writer of song must build his composition and the director of plays for the theater must produce his show. The actor's and the stage director's drive toward a sensationally effective performance that will endure with time depends on the quality of the manuscript. Stagecraft alone will not suffice. History shows the immortality of the world's greatest plays grew from their concepts and the beauty of their language, not the histrionic performance. It is the writer's responsibility and his opportunity to create meaning and emotion through dialogue vibrating with clearly audible and highly intelligible sounds. He cannot afford to overlook any chance to charge his language with auditory power and sensuous feeling, because there lie the circuits and feedbacks of the mind's ear. Phonetic signals have, up to now, been neglected. Their potential effectiveness is yet to be developed. Their ramified connections with the mind's eye, logic, and emotional networks can yield more power to the imaginative writer and the word technician.

4

The Striking Powers of Words

THE WORD "RED" MAY REFER TO A COLOR CLASSIFICATION, TO A political movement, to rage—"seeing red," or to a financial statement, "in the red." The verb "to see" may mean to observe; to accompany a person—"see her to the door"; to meet or converse with—"Mr. X will see Mr. Y."; to investigate—"see if the motor works"; to experience—"see service"; to discern— "she sees the truth," or, "they see the light"; to assume responsibility—"he's going to see about that." These examples show how numerous and different are the overlapping shades of meaning that isolated words convey, and why word-signals are frequently ambiguous.

The doctor, the scientist, the engineer, and other specialists eliminate the ambiguities inherent in words when they establish a technical vocabulary for their own use. They deliberately pin words down to point toward specific things. Their technical vocabulary intentionally eradicates all the fiction, the auras of feeling, the multiple associations, and the double talk that tradition, emotion, and imagination weave around words. Then words cease to connote; they denote.

The writer's attitude toward words is different. He is the only specialist who has a technical interest in the sensory penumbras, the imaginative associations, and the emotional tones of words. These interests derive from the functions of writing to evoke or illuminate feelings and desires, to influence men to act (which depends more on emotion than on logic), to describe and verify tastes and ideas, and to enlarge the imagination so it can either escape reality or focus more sharply upon it. These services, especially the emotive, evocative, and imaginative ones, may be aided by the multiple meanings carried in the vocabularies of everyday spech. They may be concise to intensify or expansive to reveal, but never do they formally define experience. When a writer reconstructs events verbally, his words are the connective tissues of memorable experience. This task forces every writer to have some experimental interest in the enrichment and refinement of language.

The effect of the timbre of the voice is almost tactile, as though the texture of the organs of speech touched the nerves in the inner ear. The timbre of words has limited usage. The casts of the voice give over-all impressions. They do not lend themselves easily to isolation. It is difficult to separate timbre values and arrange them in clear-cut patterns. The three most controllable factors for building up phonetic patterns are the power, the tone, and the time characteristics in the sounds of everyday words. These physical properties have a cumulative effect in the syllables, words, and phrases through which the writer "talks" to the "reading listener" when he peruses the printed page.

Since an orator or an actor can whisper a word or shout the same word with a dramatic effect sixty times as loud, it is obvious that written language cannot and should not be concerned with the extreme variations of interpretive speech. The rhythmic accents that a writer can write into or set in his language are the relative phonetic powers inherent in words when spoken with the loudness of normal conversational speech, i.e., at a

60-decibel level. Then the scanning of the accents of words becomes a judgment of how their intrinsic phonetic powers will probably affect the hearing of the average reader or listener. Such judgments depend on a sense of probability. They estimate the tendencies of words and syllables to be spoken with more or less auditory prominence, i.e., conspicuousness to the ear. Accordingly, the capacities of syllables and words to command auditory attention is the meaning of their "striking power."

Figure 5 (see page 45) is a comparative picture of the relative striking powers of sounds used in speech. These constitute the basis for the sections on the striking powers of the sounds of speech in the acoustic tables in Part II of this book.

The striking powers of the individual sounds of speech were evaluated in syllables whose tone levels and time durations were constant. The striking power numbers are numerical positions in an order of increasing striking powers relative to one convenient unit. This unit is the striking power of the sound of *th* in *thin*, taken as 1. Because *th* is the weakest sound and is given Number 1, the striking power numbers of the stronger sounds are solely indications of their striking powers relative to *th*.

You will observe, after studying Figure 5, that most of the consonants have approximately the same value; so do the vowels. There are conspicuous exceptions such as in the quick little grunting sound of ə in *the* and in a few "weak sister" vowel sounds such as o͞o, o͝o, ĭ, ĕ. The semivowels *r*, *l*, *w* and the percussive hiss *ch* as in *choo-choo* sound stronger than the average consonant. This simplification gives us a guide for considering the power of many words, but not all. *The greater the number or density of consonants in a syllable, the greater the striking power.* For example: compare (see Fig. 4) the sounds *I, tie, try, strive, strives*. One factor in the power differences of these words, each of which contains the same vowel, is that their loudness increases as their time dimension increases.

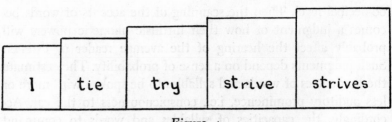

Figure 4

Because each articulated consonant contributes its own striking power to the syllable that contains it, the striking power number of a syllable is the sum total of the striking power numbers of its vowels and its consonants. Naturally, nonarticulated sounds such as the *w* in *whole* are not counted.

Figure 6 shows graphic comparisons of extremely weak and strong single-syllable words in the light of their relative striking powers on the ear. They are arranged in phrases. The numbers are the values of the relative striking powers of syllables and words, calculated from the table included in Figure 5.

Figure 7 is an example of words arranged in a sentence.

There are three distinct levels of striking power that the ear can discriminate in the sentence, *The tea was warm and clear.* If this sentence had been *the tea was made warm and clear,* a keenly sensitive ear might detect four levels of word power; the striking-power value of *made* is 34 and lies between *tea* and *warm*. These techniques make three and occasionally four degrees of the loudness in conversational speech available to the writer.

The antique methods of "scanning" taught in English classes today do not discriminate loudness from time duration or from tonality. That is why, decades ago, the great British acoustician, E. W. Scripture, ridiculed the so-called iambic, troche, dactyllic meters of language as "a fantastic fabric of fancy without the faintest foundation in fact."

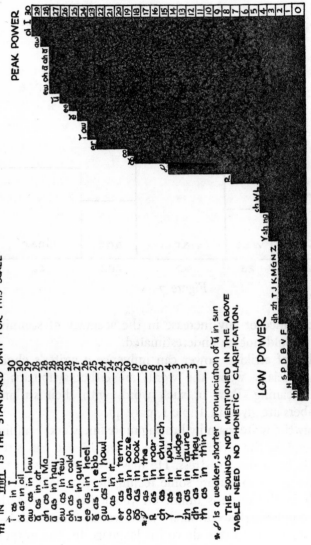

THE HEARD STRIKING POWER OF SOUNDS USED IN CONVERSATIONAL SPEECH

th IN thin IS THE STANDARD UNIT FOR THIS SCALE

ī as in I	30
oi as in oil	30
aw as in law	29
ā as in at	28
ah oo in Ma	28
ā as in hay	28
ew as in few	28
oh as in cold	28
ŭ as in gun	27
ee as in heel	26
ĕ as in ebb	25
ōu as in howl	24
ı as in it	24
er as in term	23
oo as in ooze	20
ŏŏ as in book	19
*ᴊ as in the	15
R as in roar	8
ch as in church	5
Y as in you	4
j as in judge	3
zh as in azure	3
dh as in they	3
th as in thin	1

* ᴊ is a weaker, shorter pronunciation of ŭ in sun

THE SOUNDS NOT MENTIONED IN THE ABOVE
TABLE NEED NO PHONETIC CLARIFICATION.

PEAK POWER

LOW POWER

Figure 5

The striking power values of the consonants are based on the determinations of their relative intensity in decibels by Harvey Fletcher.

The values for vowels and diphthongs considered the different sensitivities of hearing to different tones, and the effects of time duration on loudness.

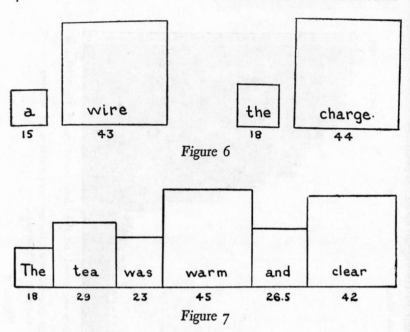

Figure 6

Figure 7

The importance of any increase in the accuracy of scanning techniques should not be underestimated.

Knowledge of striking power can influence a writer's choice of words, especially when the words are either synonyms or overlap in meaning. Pairs of such words with their striking-power numbers are given in Table 1, page 47.

What may the writer gain by hearing more finely and handling more deliberately the striking powers of words? He can stress the thoughts he wishes to stress. He may use variations in the power of his words to feature some feeling he especially desires to establish in the reader's mind. Or the writer may use the method of employing exceptionally weak words, those with low striking-power value, to step down his language for the purpose of contrast; or he may use hushed words for appropriate moods. Noticeable shifts in the flow of verbal power can suggest subtle

TABLE 1. STRIKING-POWER NUMBERS OF PAIRED WORDS

46 strike	28.5 hit
44 large	29 big
37 shall	25 should
35 smell	29 24 o(d)(d)or (d shared by syllables)
44 short	30.5 6.5 li(t)(t)le (t shared by syllables)
39 placed	24 put
47 strange	23 new
35 well	23 good

and delicate changes in the intensity of emotion and the impacts of things on our consciousness. The technique may be considered as an "ear punctuation" to clarify ideas, feelings, and emotions. When the writer uses this kind of punctuation he edges his thoughts with acoustic contours that make his words more effective.

From a strictly technical viewpoint, a grasp and mastery of the power of words gives the writer a valuable instrument. It is rhythm. There are phonetic billows in discernible waves when the power bursts of words move in perceptible periods of time. Word rhythms with the pulse of power can create style. They may express feelings, forms, and the motions of things. These are the potential values of the information contained in the phonetic tables in Part II. But here, as in all other applications of these auditory instruments, the way they are used is the supreme test. Do they release feelings and intuitions that require new words because the conventional ones are inadequate? Do they set up patterns for composition? Do they suggest literary form? Do they eliminate bad writing in the light of analysis? Will they sell soap, or lead to the inspiration of an ideal language of feeling?

The answers depend on the creative abilities of the writer and on his interests.

The writer's interests as a reporter have not been mentioned. The reportorial service verbalizes acts and facts in order to give "news." Unless a writer has an editorial or commentator status, he just reports what he sees. As a result, reportorial writing uses words as translucent references to dry facts and acts stripped as bare as possible of all their sensory and emotive associations.

Most writers are faced with the problem of communicating to people thin in experience. The understanding of the acoustic ticketing and the signaling jobs of words depends on the experience of the reader-listener with the subject of the words. This is an obvious fact, but its implications are not. For, if we admit that the references of words are richer or poorer according to a person's experience with the things referred to, then the specialized manufacturing, engineering, and scientific knowledge incorporated in the majority of the objects in our environment today makes most of us ignorant—verbally as well as otherwise. This trend increases. The ever-extending specializations of our age are removing a growing number of things and processes beyond the scope of verbal comprehension. The gains in society's collective knowledge outpace the understanding of the individual. The word tags attached to the numerous valves and gears in an automobile motor are meaningless to the average driver without mechanical or engineering backgrounds in the automotive fields. "Decibel," "ionization," "radiation pressure" are incomprehensible sounds without knowledge of the physical measurements and the mathematical relations these words refer to. Therefore, the denotative use of words to report "facts," as though words were colorless, transparent windows, applies to shrinking regions of experience and limits the scope of the writer. Now, more than ever, the writer and our technological society need to enrich the citizen's subjective world with a new vocabulary of feeling.

5

Whisper Tones
in Words

NEXT IN IMPORTANCE TO THE DYNAMIC POWER OF LANGUAGE sounds is their tone. The reader may recall that the vowels presented in the orchestra of the language, Figure 2, were grouped into three classes: low, middle, and high tone. There was a reason for this arrangement. It is easier for the ear to detect differences in tone between low, middle, and high vowels than to make tonal distinctions among vowels within the same group. Inspection of the vowel scale in Figure 8 shows why this is the case. Vowel tones within the same register are not located far below or above one another. The entire scale is presented in Figure 8, with the exception of a few sounds that are slight modifications of those given, and therefore are not significant. Since the diphthongs oi in noise, ew in few, and ī in I are fusions of primary vowels, the only true middle-tone vowel sound is ah in father. (Figure 8, The Vowel Scale.)

The rise of the vowel scale can be heard if the reader will whisper aloud, without affectation, this sequence of names: June, Joan, John, Jane, Jean. The fall in tones will be noticed by whispering, again in a natural manner: Jean, Jane, John, Joan, June. Whispering eliminates the resonance of the vocal chords and

VOWEL SCALE

The range of the numbers on this scale and their spacing were calibrated to be used with the striking power of words that tend to vary between 25 and 45.

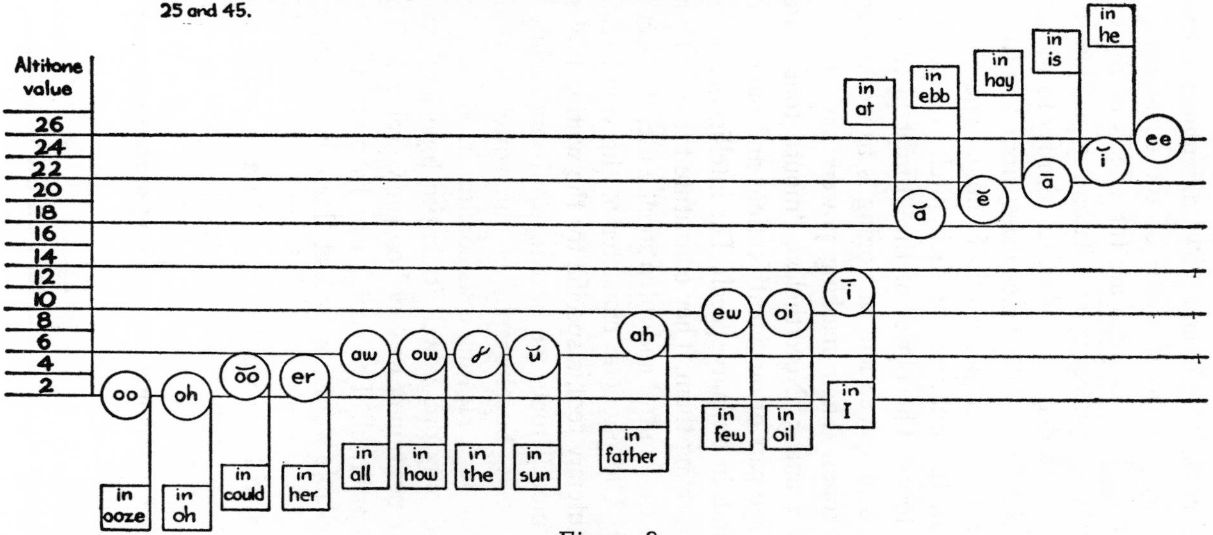

Altitone value	
26	
24	
22	
20	
18	
16	
14	
12	
10	
8	
6	
4	
2	

ee — in he
i — in is
ā — in hay
e — in ebb
ă — in at

ī — in I
oi — in oil
ew — in few
oh — in father

ŭ — in sun
θ — in the
ow — in how
aw — in all
er — in her
oo — in could
oh — in oh
oo — in ooze

Figure 8

51

shows that the "high" and "low" differences in tone are created entirely by changes in shape of the chambers in the mouth. These oral shape changes are the effects of the curling, humping, dropping, spreading, and flattening positions of the tongue. In case the reader has doubts, let him try to whisper Jean, Jane, John, Joan, June with tones rising from low to high. It is impossible. On the other hand, if chordal and throatal vibrations do occur, the influence of their pitch is superimposed on the mouth tones. The power of the "throat pitch" in shouted intonations of speech and in singing is to weaken our hearing of mouth tones. Their masking powers have been suggested in Figures 3 and 5. Nevertheless, "mouth tones" are responsible for a huge part of our identifications and our discriminations of the sounds in ordinary speech. The intelligence of words depends on recognizing them. They constitute the only tonal values that a writer can control and intentionally use, to affect the reader or listener. The phonetic character of the vowel scale makes it a strictly literary tool, a specific for the writing profession.

The mouth tones we hear in words are mainly the tones of their vowels. Spectographs of the vowel overtones in words prove this fact. Hearing tests confirm it. When a word contains one and only one vowel, its entire tone level will rise or fall with the position of its vowel on the vowel scale. This simplification is practical. The writer can listen to the tone levels of single-syllable words, or look at them, just as though they were vowels on the vowel scale. This applies to any syllable, whether it occurs within a word or constitutes a whole word. Figure 9 is a representation of how the tone levels of words rise with the altitude of their vowels on the vowel scale. When the reader whispers these words in the rising order shown on the scale, he will hear their tones ascend.

Figure 10 shows a sequence of names in an order that shows a continuous rise or fall of tone on the vowel scale.

53

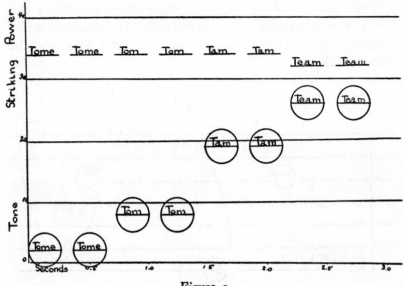

Figure 9

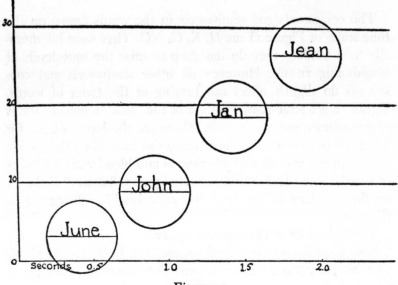

Figure 10

The tones in polysyllabic words rise and fall with the vowel levels of their syllables on the vowel scale. The words shown in Figure 11 are examples: *cooker, hanging, going, inky,* and the name, *Kankakee.*

Polysyllabic

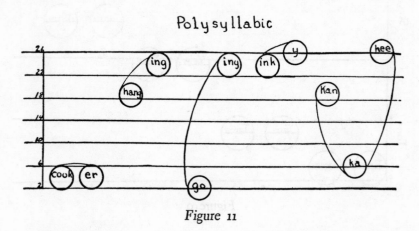

Figure 11

The consonants and semivowels in the words drawn on the tone scales of Figure 11 are *H, K, G, NG.* They were intentionally used because they do not drop or raise the tone levels of neighboring vowels. However, all other semivowels and consonants do slightly affect our hearing of the tones of words. Figure 12 is a scale representation of the "tone influence" levels of consonants and semivowels. These are the levels where, for a fraction of a second, we hear changes in tone when the sounds of consonants and semivowels flow in and blend with the tones of vowels. The slight extent of these "tone influences" is shown by the positions of words in the copy headline illustrated in Figure 12.

The tone drift of the words is upward.

New contains the low level oo and the high semivowel *N.* The *N* raises the oo tone of new, just above the Number 2

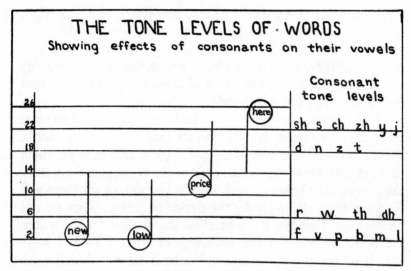

Figure 12

level which the vowel *oo* would otherwise occupy on the vowel scale.

Low is composed of the vowel *oh* and the semivowel *l*. Both are on the same tone level. This causes the tone altitude of *low* to have exactly the same tone height as its vowel *oh*. When *oh* is neither lifted nor dropped in tone by consonants or adjacent semivowels, it holds to the same Number 2 scale position as an unmodified *oo*. Therefore, if you listen attentively to several of your own whisperings of *new* and *low*, you will hear that *new* sounds slightly higher than *low*.

The word *price* contains the low semivowel *r* and the high consonant *s*. Their altitudes are approximately the same distance above and below the level of the *i* in *price*. Because they occur in the short time interval of a single syllable, they neutralize their opposite impressions on our hearing of height in tone. The result is that we hear the altitone of *price* as though it were unaffected by either its consonant or semivowel. Its tonal height is the one occupied by its diphthong *i* on the vowel scale.

The vowel *ee* in *here* is not noticeably affected by *h* because *h* is one of those consonants whose articulation does not modify vowel tones. However, *r* is low. Therefore, *here* lies a half a unit below the *ee* on the vowel scale.

These examples confirm what *The Orchestra of the Language* previously illustrated. It's the vowels that give tone to words. Consonants and semivowels may blur tonal effects, make them decisive with the timbre in the casts of the voice, give them striking power, shift tones up and down a fraction, or set tones and fix them more definitely by the device of rhyme. They do not create tone. This fact has a practical implication for the writer. He need not consider the influences of consonants and semivowels on the tones of words unless he is interested in the minute refinements of auditory affects and feeling.

The tones of words may be used by the writer to enhance the emotional stories he wishes to tell. Use of the vowel scale will aid the writer in creating tone rhythms with words, refinement of rhyme, language music, euphony of style; and it will help him brighten or darken his expressions of feeling. Low vowels tend to have a depressing effect; high ones frequently leave a bright, stimulating impression. "The gloom of polar cold" is depressive in language tone as well as in fact and feeling.

One of the most perfect expressions of human despair is the famous line from *Macbeth:* "Tomorrow and tomorrow and tomorrow." A tone portrayal of the words in this line is presented in Figure 13.

The overwhelming low tone of the whole line and the repetitive rhythm of the words convey a sense of monotonous depression that characterizes utter hopelessness. The tone patterns carried by the words tell the same emotional story that the ordinary meaning of the words communicates. Shakespeare reinforced his message to the audience with auditory intelligence.

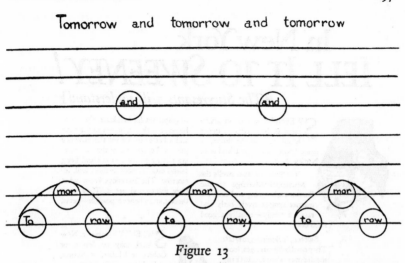

Figure 13

The suggestion was projected, at the end of Chapter IV, that the striking powers of words can be used as "ear-punctuations" to give edge and acoustic contour to the feelings and ideas of the writer. A line like "Tomorrow and tomorrow and tomorrow" shows how tone patterns also may point up the meanings of words. Nor need we restrict ourselves to Shakespearean poetry to hear the rhythms of tones on the vowel scale. They sharpen the most common of everyday expressions.

"Tell it to Sweeney" is a brush-off signal that expresses impatience and annoyance. It may communicate a contemptuous sort of skepticism. The highness and the shrillness of the two ee sounds in Sweeney and the tension in the vocal chords to articulate them are fitting accompaniments to the mood. The forms of the movements of the tongue in pronouncing "Tell it to Sweeney" suggest a brush-off gesture. "Tell it to Thomson," "Tell it to Cohen," or Muller, or Nelson, or La Voie feature lower-toned names. They are not as effective. The "tone-assist" has vanished. The tongue pantomime no longer echoes the emotions in the phrase.

In New York
TELL IT TO SWEENEY!
{The Stuyvesants will understand}

SWEENEY lives in an apartment in Brooklyn, on upper Manhattan, in the Bronx, or has a house on Staten Island or in Nutley, N. J.

It is Sweeney who swells the Municipal Marriage License Bureau each spring and fall. He marries comparatively early and raises a family—usually a good sized one.

Sweeney's children grow fast: They need baby carriages, foods, medicines, shoes, clothing, books, pianos, bathing suits, Christmas trees, tonsilotomy, tuition, trousseaux, phonograph records—in fact, everything.

Sweeney's sons filled both rear and front ranks in the late war; some of them stood ahead of the ranks. They drive trucks, belong to trade unions, work in offices, sell goods and run businesses.

Sweeney's daughters go to school, some of them to college; some of them work in factories, pound typewriters, sell retail merchandise, design Paris frocks. Eventually 75% of them marry.

* * *

SWEENEY and Mrs. Sweeney are ambitious and expectant of Life. They believe in God, the United States and life insurance. They respect education, and want the kids to have plenty of it. They look forward to grapefruit for breakfast, their own homes, a little car, money in the bank and a better future for the Sweeney juniors. Today some of the Sweeneys are buying Pierce Arrows and Long Island estates; more of them will, tomorrow. The Sweeneys know what they want—and get it. They *want the best*, and whenever possible—get it.

* * *

SWEENEY'S name in New York may be Smith, or Cohen, or Muller, or Nelson, or La Voie—or Sweeney.

There are a million families of Sweeneys in and around New York, with incomes from $6,000 *down*.

You men who aspire to sell large bills of goods to New York, remember the Sweeneys. They comprise 75% of any large city's population. Address your advertising, your sales messages, to them, because they are your best customers. They keep right on living and dying, earning and spending money, buying and using merchandise. They are not hard to sell, and they *are* good folks to do business with. And remember, when you talk to Sweeney, the people of bluer blood and more money who read The News will understand; whereas if you talk to Stuyvesants, the Sweeneys won't listen. You can't lose by saying it so Sweeney understands.

TELL It to Sweeney—in The News, bought by more than *two-fifths* of all the people in New York City who buy an English language morning newspaper.

Courtesy of The News, New York City.

Figure 14

To what degree unconscious phonetic intelligence influenced the ordinary Joe aptly to select Sweeney, among all the other possible names, is one of those questions no one can answer. A copy of the famous advertisement that traded on "Tell it to Sweeney" as an attention-getting gimmick is presented in Figure 14. The technique of startling the reader was effected by unexpectedly using this slang gesture literally, as though it had no emotional associations. Before the reader's mind had adjusted, the emotion in the headline led him into the copy. The lure worked. Sweeney was promoted to immortality "among the nightingales."

Phrases such as "Don't say beer . . . Say Schlitz," "Now go get Pepsi," "Don't wait . . . for a party . . . serve it . . . tonight," strike rising tone rhythms that give a phonetic lift to the stimulus and the lilt that the words intend to induce in the imagination of prospective customers.

If you pronounce the ĕ in red and the ĭ in it rapidly enough to fuse them in a single sound, that sound is the diphthong ā in say: (ĕ → ĭ = ā). When words or syllables featuring the diphthong ā in say are rapidly succeeded or preceded by words or syllables stressing the component vowels ĕ in red and ĭ in it they produce tonal beats; i.e., "Fresh spring rain," "Say it again," "Elfin face." Repetition augments the effect. Here is the key to the melody in the punch phrase of one of the most popular jingles of our era: "Say it again . . . Virginia Dare." As shown here the diphthong tones are ringed and the vowel accents are marked in a phonetic presentation of the phrase:

S(ā)y (ĭ)t ə g(ĕ)·n . . . V e r g(ĭ)n y ə D(ĕ)ə r

Notice how the short, low-toned vowel ə as in the assists in giving a tonal lift to key syllables and words that contain higher vowels. And observe how this weakest of syllables, ə, develops the striking power values or accents that enhance the tonal beat in key words.

The technique for making tonal beats with the diphthong ā in *say* applies to other diphthongs such as ī in *bite*: (ī = ah → ĭ); *oi* in *noise* (oi = aw → ĭ); *ow* in *howl* (ow = ah → ŏŏ); *ew* in *few* (ew = ĭ → ŏŏ). The underlying principle for this technique is to lift several recessive tones over the threshold of hearing. They, the recessive vowels (tones we do not consciously hear), are made audible by repeating them alongside a dominant vowel tone (the tone we do consciously hear), which contains the recessives as parts of itself. The same principle holds for vowels that are not diphthongs. Any vowel whose dominant and recessive overtones are spoken in rapid succession produces a tonal beat. The auditory effect is analogous to the tonal carry-over we hear when two piano notes that possess the same overtone are played in swift succession. It so happens that the vowel *ee* in *green* has a recessive overtone which constitutes the dominant tone of the vowel *oo* in *noon*. Briefly, the tone of *oo* is an overtone of *ee*. In consequence, a repeated voicing of these two vowels in a succession of names and words such as *Lucille, Louise, keen tools, green pools* gives tonal beats. One of the most popular songs in the 1920's, "Tea for Two," features this vowel rhythm.

The euphonious effects of vowel tone beats are melodic. If repeated frequently enough in short intervals of time they may be clearly heard. Then they contribute a musical quality to language. The tonal beats of vowels can be serviceable to writers of jingles, songs, librettos, poetry, and advertising copy. But tonal beats not give the lift or the emotionally depressive affects that tonal patterns do. An indication of the importance of the signaling power of pattern is that tone patterns can be used in prose to convey feeling. If one listens attentively to the steady fall of word tones in the phrase, "She, grieving, sat among cold rooms," one's auditory intelligence detects a tonal curve descending to the lowest level. One senses that the orientation of this curve corresponds to the story of the emotion. An audi-

tory shadow, moving with time from word to word, has added
some information to the referential meaning of a sentence.
Figure 15 shows the graph of this tonal pattern.

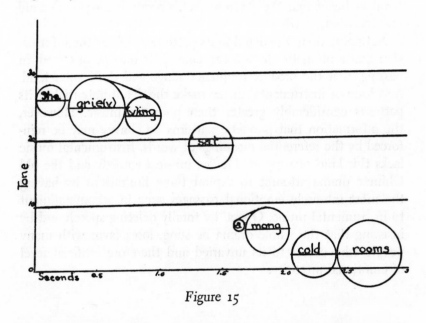

Figure 15

The service of pattern to the writer of phonetic music is just
as crucial as the contribution of form to the composer of instrumental music. But the writer of phonetic music with words
faces an additional problem. Will the low-loudness level of
language render his music inaudible? Repetition is a common
trick for overcoming this problem. But repetition is the most
primitive form of rhythm. Concisely, rhythm is any order that
we recognize as a function of time. Only when a rhythm possesses more variety of structure or pattern will its capacity for
intelligence be enlarged. From this outlook, primitive repetition
is only one special case of rhythm. The more the time, the tone,
the loudness, and the timbre fluctuate, the greater the number

of possible shapes in a sound rhythm's form, and the greater its potential for pattern detail. One of the contributions of these techniques is to liberate the mind of the writer from the habit or belief that the rhythms of his prose or prosody depend on repetition.

Naturally, then, the detail in its pattern will limit the information that a phonetic rhythm can convey. It may be observed, in passing, that the broader frequency range and the greater loudness level of instrumental music make the detail potential of its patterns considerably greater than phonetic music. However, the information that phonetic patterns do convey may be reinforced by the referential meanings of words. Instrumental music lacks this kind of support. Hence, musical comedy and the old Chinese drama attempt to exploit these limitations by having the most intensely emotional passages sung in accompaniment to instrumental music. Opera, by totally deleting speech and by insisting that the whole drama be sung, loses favor with many people who object to its unvaried and therefore artificial level of emotional intensity.

6

The Time Dimension of
Words and Syllables

WHEN A WRITER WISHES TO FOLLOW THE NATURAL POWER OR
tone pattern of a phrase or sentence, he should visualize the
rhythms of the pattern taking shape while a person reads or
talks. That is, he should evaluate their continuity in time. For
this purpose, the average duration of words will suffice. Also,
the natural flow of speech, which a writer wishes to put into his
sentences, must be based on the average speaker, not on an
unusually fast or slow speaker. An illustration of the sounds of
average American speech with the time duration given in seconds is shown in Figure 17 (see page 65).

The words of shortest duration in most common use are: *a,
the, trip, out, pick, check, put, did, could, what, it.* When the
vowels in the words "in" and "to" are pronounced with the short
grunt of the vowel in *the,* then they are among the shortest
words. Combinations of short vowels and percussion consonants
produce rapid words. These can be made by selecting the shortest time duration phonemes that appear in Table 3 in Part II.

The staccato consonants that give speed to these words have
another value. Their abruptness and sharpness cause the listener

to be more attentive. They permit the ear, for reasons not completely understood, to hear sounds at a lower decibel level.

In Figure 16 are quantitative comparisons of words of extremely long and short durations.

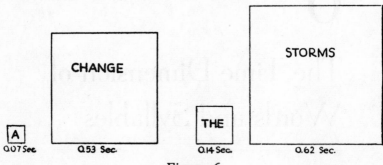

Figure 16

There is a way to create monosyllabic words with great duration and single syllables that extend over a long period of time. The technique is simple. Build words with the long diphthongs ī, ew, oi, and ā, and surround these prolonged sounds with the maximum number of consonants. Table 2 illustrates this technique

TABLE 2. DURATION OF MONOSYLLABIC WORDS

Words Containing Diphthongs			
	ire	rise	crimes
Sec.	0.29	0.43	0.55
	our	rouse	growls
Sec.	0.29	0.43	0.60
	oil	soil	broils
Sec.	0.29	0.41	0.60
	ape	spain	sprains
Sec.	0.29	0.48	0.62

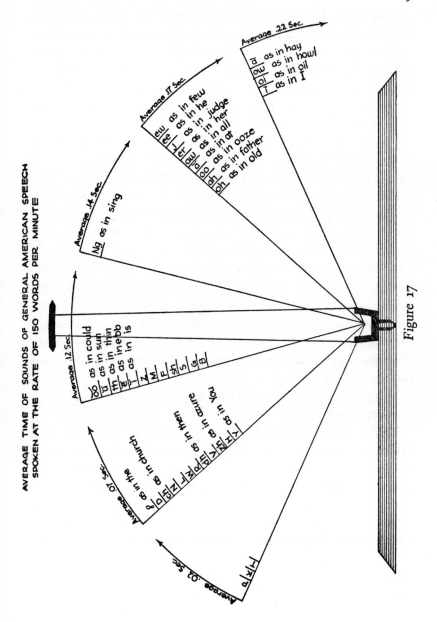

AVERAGE TIME OF SOUNDS OF GENERAL AMERICAN SPEECH
SPOKEN AT THE RATE OF 150 WORDS PER MINUTE

Figure 17

This table illustrates how the duration of words will grow when the number or density of consonants and semivowels increases. If we stop to think about this fact for a moment, it is obvious. Some speaking time is consumed in articulating a consonant or semivowel. Accordingly, the greater the number of consonants or semivowels in a syllable or word, the greater the amount of time consumed by it.

Questions will arise about the validity of these durations of words when they are read from the printed page. It is well known that the reader's eyes will skip letters while he reads. He will skip words, too. These are facts. But the writer cannot know in advance which letters the reader will skip any more than he can predict which words will remain unread. A writer must assume that what he writes will be read. Otherwise, he would not put his words down on paper. Furthermore, today few writers can be certain that their creations will not be given, at some future date, over the air, the video, or in motion pictures. Therefore, the average time of conversation is the practical standard for estimating the durations of words. Let the reader test these statements by considering his own time-feelings when he reads the words in Table 2.

Table 3 will give the writer the range of the duration of words in more detail.

Tables 2 and 3 show that the short words extend in time through approximately one fourth of a second, the long words through six tenths of a second. Medium duration ones last between a third and a half of a second. When words such as *us* and *it* are slurred, their vowels sound like the ə in *the* and their time durations are cut down to 0.19 seconds and 0.14 seconds. This analysis shows there are three, and occasionally four, degrees of word-time discrimination available to the writer. The time distinctions among words offered by this technique are the same in degree as the striking power differences.

TABLE 3. EFFECT OF DIPHTHONGS, AVERAGE VOWELS, AND SHORT
VOWELS ON DURATION OF MONOSYLLABLES

	One Con-sonant or Semivowel	WORDS WITH: Three Con-sonants and/ or Semivowels	Five Con-sonants and/ or Semivowels
Diphthongs	age 0.39 sec. ice 0.34	stage 0.53 sec. fights 0.48	strange 0.67 strifes 0.67
Average Vowels	ear 0.24 oar 0.24	dream 0.40 store 0.38	screams 0.62 storms 0.62
Short Vowels	it 0.19 us 0.24	lint 0.28 rust 0.33	splint 0.42 strums 0.57

There is also a tendency for the last syllable in a phrase or
sentence to prolong its duration about one third of average
speaking time. This tendency is probably due to the habits of
average American speech. It has been mentioned that this extra
duration will make terminal syllables and words more conspicuous to the ear and that this may be one of the physical factors
that stabilize the rhythms of both end-rhyme and free verse.
Singers take advantage of this extra and natural time extension
to hold the note longer. That is why the "stop percussions" consonants such as k, t, p, ch, which break down resonance, seldom
terminate the line of a song on a long-held note. The word
"seldom" is used advisedly, because the lyricist occasionally may
wish to break the resonance for various reasons. This example

again emphasizes that the intentions of the writer will determine the use of these instruments, and not mechanical formulas.

Up to this point monosyllabic words and single syllables have been considered. The speaking time of a series of one-syllable words is the sum of the time periods consumed by each word plus the time taken up by pauses between the words. Polysyllabic words are shorter because there are no pauses between syllables. The sounds of separate syllables imperceptibly glide into and blend with each other. Popular song writers have sensed this fact for decades. A vocabulary of multisyllable words is an important part of the artful lyricist's equipment. Pauses within sentences amount to roughly one fourth of the total

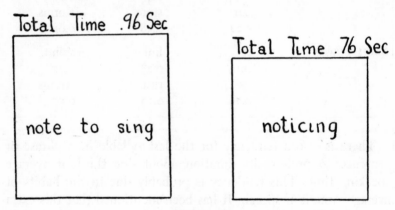

Figure 18

reading time. The elapsed time of a pause between two sentences approximates 0.65 seconds. Figure 18 compares the time factor of one-syllable words with polysyllabic words containing practically the identical sounds.

The reader will observe that it takes him less time to say the word *altimeter* than "Al to meet her" in the sentence "Was Al to meet her?"

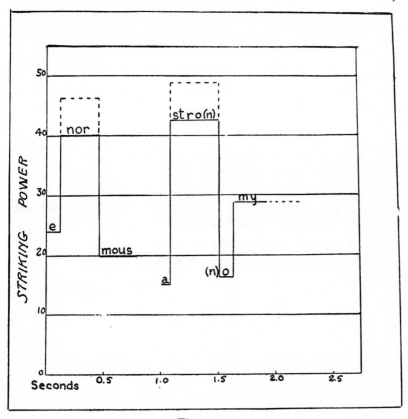

Figure 19

Because the pauses among syllables of polysyllabic words are eliminated, a speaker tends to slur the unaccented syllables and to concentrate vocal power on one syllable. Which one of several syllables shall receive this extra stress is a matter of convention. When the accent of convention does fall on a syllable, the power of this accent is an addition to the normal striking power of that syllable. Experimentation shows that this increment of power approximates 6 on the scale of striking power numbers. Accordingly, the focusing of vocal power on a conventionally stressed syllable will be revealed by dotted lines. The increment of 6 will give the striking power patterns of polysyllabic words a greater fidelity to hearing. The dots placed above the undotted striking power line demonstrate the fact of a conventional accent. This information can be useful to song writers. Figure 19 is a graph of this effect.

There is stimulation and exhaustion in the nerves of the inner ear while we listen to speech. And there are rhythms of attention by listeners. These are the broader considerations behind the fact that readers and audiences do react, more or less consciously, to the start-stop, start-stop time rhythms of phrases and sentences. Knowledge of the relative durations of words and pauses in the flow of speech will give the writer a keener control and a new power to make his phrases and sentences more readable, more rhythmic, and more significant.

7

Power-Tone Patterns and the Influence of Time

LET US CONSIDER TWO SENTENCES WHOSE RHYTHMS DEPEND almost entirely on variations in the vocal power of the words. The first sentence is: "We tripped a sharpster." The second is: "We outguessed that crook." Now, let us chart the rise and fall in the striking power of all the syllables and words in the two sentences. We shall use a scale that runs from zero to fifty. The number given to each syllable or word on the scale is the sum of the striking power numbers of every sound in a syllable or word. These numbers appear in the striking power table and graph shown in Figure 5. They are also given in Tables 1 and 4 in Part II of this book. It is obvious that a syllable with a larger striking power number will appear higher up on the scale than one with a smaller number. These fluctuations in height enable the writer to scan the rise and fall of the power of words in a sentence. Figure 20 presents the striking-power rhythms of "We tripped a sharpster" and "We outguessed that crook."

The time extensions of syllables or words can also be graphically drawn, and the relative lengths of their durations can be numerically given in seconds. The calculation of the duration for a word follows the same method used to give striking power

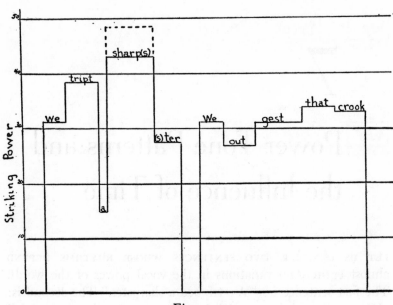

Figure 20

numbers to words. The time duration of a syllable or a whole word is the sum of the duration of all the sounds articulated in the speaking of the word. The average number of seconds for all the durations of all the sounds of general American speech were presented in Figure 17. They appear in Part II in Tables 2 and 3. Figure 21 illustrates the extensions in seconds of every syllable in "We tripped a sharpster," and "We outguessed that crook." The time intervals within the former sentence show greater differences and therefore lack the regularity of the durations of the syllables in the second sentence. The even spacing of the word time in the latter contributes to it a sense of deliberateness that the first sentence lacks. The writer should make the auditory observation that "tripped" and "outguessed" are pronounced "trĭpt" and "outgĕst" and that the power and time numbers on the graph of Figure 22 have been calculated

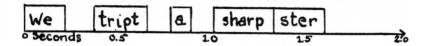

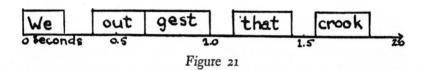

Figure 21

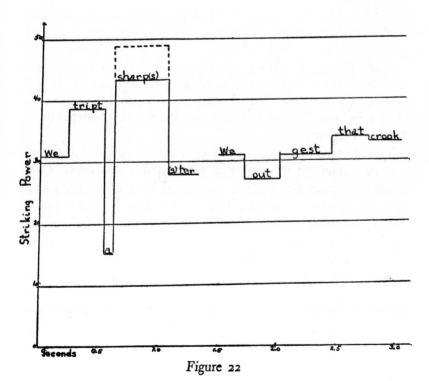

Figure 22

phonetically on the basis of their most probable pronunciation.

From this point on, instead of picturing the powers and durations of words or syllables on separate diagrams, we are going to portray them on a single graph. The labor saved is obvious. At a glance, the writer can inspect one drawing and interpret the time and power rhythms carried by the sounds of speech in his written words. We shall call the moving sound tracks of word power that fluctuate with speaking time *the dynamic rhythm of writing.* The graph of Figure 22 shows the dynamic rhythm of "We tripped a sharpster" and "We outguessed that crook." When the patterns of these sentences are compared, it becomes clear that the differences between the altitudes of syllabic plateaus on dynamic graphs show the degrees of change in the power of words. These differences give us a technique for sharpening the power rhythms of words: flank the peaks of power with the weakest syllable or words. The low valleys make the high points jut. "We tripped a sharpster" has a more definitive dynamic rhythm than "We outguessed that crook." It is a sharper expression, and its bouncy, wavier rhythm suggests a livelier feeling. "We outguessed that crook" is, phonetically, a flatter statement.

The plateaus in dynamic patterns show the approximate duration in seconds of the power of each syllable and word. They reveal the differences in time consumed by words spoken at a rate of 150 words a minute. They do not show pauses between phrases and words within a sentence that consume close to 0.25 seconds of speaking time. A pause within a sentence extends about the same period of time as to pronounce an average single-syllable word. Figure 22 shows that the time rhythm of "We outguessed that crook" is less broken than the rhythm of "We tripped a sharpster." The duration ratios support the power patterns of both sentences, the flatness of the former and the jaggedness of the latter.

Why aren't the pauses within sentences specified in audio-

scriptic patterns? In the first place, commas, colons, and exclamation marks are punctuational commands to pause. If these
do not suffice, the writer can designate intrasentence pauses
with dots . . . or—he can use a dash. There are two arrangements
of words that can create pauses without the artifice of punctuational barbs. One is poetry, especially free verse. The other is
advertising copy. These arts fabricate pauses by converting a
phrase, or even a lone word, into a single sentence. This effect
depends partly on the tendency of the voice to pause between
two sentences for approximately 0.6 seconds at a speech rate
of 150 words per minute. The technique is enhanced by the
previously mentioned habit of English speech to increase the
duration of the terminal syllable of a sentence by roughly one
third. And the eye, in passing from line to line, consumes some
reading time.

The plateaus on dynamic graphs do not show the time for
building up the peaks of power nor for the decay of power in
the phonetic waves within syllables and words. These risings
and fall-offs of power occur in such minute intervals of time that
the value of this information to the writer is questionable.
Although the extensions of plateaus on dynamic graphs do reveal the time durations of word power within a sentence, they
do not show the periods of time required to speak entire sentences. This can be done. All that is necessary is to add the time
required to speak each word in a phrase or sentence. . . . Then
take these total durations or periods and graph them on a scale
calibrated to fit the size of a page. Let us take Franklin D.
Roosevelt's opening sentence in his declaration-of-war speech
immediately after Pearl Harbor: "Yesterday . . . December
seventh, nineteen forty-one—a day that will live in infamy—the
United States of America was suddenly and deliberately attacked." It is to be observed that this long sentence is punctuated to be spoken in a series of phrases isolated by pauses.

Here is the phonetic presentation of the durations in seconds of each word in a phrase. In Figure 23, in boxes, are the total periods in seconds for each phrase.

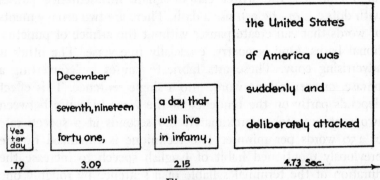

Figure 23

Yĕs ter dā — Dee sĕm ber sĕvvĕnth nīn teen fawr tĭ
0.31 0.19 0.29   0.24 0.36 0.29 0.30 0.37 0.41 0.31 0.36 0.14

wŭn — ə dā dthăt wĭl lĭv ĭn ĭn fə mĭ —
0.31   0.07 0.29 0.31 0.26 0.31 0.24 0.24 0.19 0.24

dthee Ew nīttəd Stāts əv ə mĕrrĭ kə wŭz
0.24 0.17 0.325 0.175 0.50 0.19 0.07 0.275 0.155 0.07 0.28

sŭdd'n lĭ ănd dĭ lĭb rĭt lĭ ă tăkt.
0.38 0.19 0.33 0.19 0.31 0.26 0.19 0.17 0.28

The actual sounds in the words of Figure 23 are subject to some of the normal variation in American habits of speech. Dĭ lĭb rĭt lĭ might be pronounced dee lĭb rĭt lĭ; or it could be phonated by speakers as dĭlĭbə rət lĭ or dĭ lĭb ert lĭ. Also ă tăkt at a faster rate of speech could be ətăkt. These variations make negligible differences in the total durations of phrases and sentences. Their effect on dynamic rhythms is greater, but not decisive. When the writer is compelled to make phonetic decisions he should consider the most probable and the clearest diction. For this purpose a standard dictionary will help—unless he is writing in a regional dialect. Then the sounds must be analyzed and the spelling changed.

F.D.R.'s sentence has a total duration of almost 11 seconds, which taxes the attention span of many listeners or readers. So, he breaks it up into phrases set off by pauses. Notice how "yesterday" is isolated by punctuation to dramatize the timeliness of the speech. And observe the density of the high-toned front vowels that are "screechily" intense in ə dā dthăt wĭl lĭv ĭn ĭn fə mĭ, which by means of the tensions in the vocal chords suggests the intensity of feeling appropriate to such a catastrophic event. And the same shrill phonetic intensity ends with the abrupt staccato stop of tk in "ă tăkt" to punctuate the anger in sŭdd'n lĭ ănd dĭ lĭb rĭt lĭ ă tăkt.

When the writer considers the effectiveness of the time periods of whole sentences, he should never forget this fact: the effects on hearing of the periods of speaking time in whole phrases and sentences are quite different from the impressions of the dynamic patterns of word power. Behind these differences lies one psycho-acoustic fact that every writer should fix in his mind. *Our judgments of loudness are not affected by extending the time durations of speech beyond five tenths of a second.* The brain does perceive increased amounts of loudness when the durations of single syllables and monosyllabic words extend up to limits that vary between a quarter of a second and a half of a second. We have seen in Table 3 that the durations of the most prolonged syllables and monosyllabic words do not last much longer than one half a second. Any extension of their time beyond this limit adds nothing to the striking power of words. This fact has a definite bearing on the writer's use of power patterns for auditory effects. No matter how many extra words he may add to a strong phrase or sentence, the additional verbiage contributes nothing to the peaks of acoustic power within the sentence. Repetition of a dynamic rhythm will certainly focus the reader's or listener's attention on it, and it will clarify the pattern of the rhythm. But verbosity does not increase the striking power of the individual words that constitute the pattern. It can mask them. This is one of the psycho-acoustic factors that causes terse sentences to communicate most word power. Short or exclamatory expressions such as "Night falls," "Scram," "Fire," "Black out," "Alas, poor Yorick! I knew him, Horatio": gain ear recognition and audience attention that would be lost in the phonetic scramble of long sentences. A technically trained writer knows this without analysis. He also realizes that too much of this clipped type of writing may become objectionably artificial. Accordingly, the writer who wishes to establish effective dynamic rhythms throughout prolonged sentences or paragraphs must give to the power patterns of words an audibility that is unmistakably clear. They should be composed as though they were refrains surging through his writing. Otherwise, their impacts on the ear will be drowned in the long billows of speech that make the periods of time in the rhythms of whole sentences.

The effectiveness of intrasentence rhythms has been emphasized. But this does not mean that the timing of whole sentences should be neglected. The time segmentation of sentences and phrases, broken up by pauses and punctuations, emphasizes the cycles of the writer's thought and feeling, alerts listeners and readers to pay attention to changes in meaning, and may mark fluctuations of breathing. The periods of sentences are adjustments to the attention spans of readers and listeners. A slowing down or quickening in the time rhythms of sentences can indicate excitement, interest, serenity, continuity, or dramatic climaxes in the pace of a writer's thoughts. But these variations of periods are always superimposed on the choppier rhythms of word power. Because the peak striking power of a syllable or word is limited by a 0.5-second period, and because the lengths of plateaus in the power patterns of words are functions of

time, it is difficult to judge their auditory effects without some
consideration for the periodicity of the sentences that contain
them—but the qualitative differences are there. The intrasentence dynamics of words constitute a crucial factor in the language rhythms of audio-scriptic intelligence. This is probably
what the writer W. Somerset Maugham meant when he said:
". . . words should be used not only to balance a sentence but
to balance an idea." This book would add: "and to feature emotions and feelings, and to express the rhythms of processes and
the properties of things."

Let us consider a phrase whose balance depends on an almost
equal distribution of vocal power among syllables. We will take
(Figure 24) the headline of the famous Squibb advertisement:
"The Priceless Ingredient." The sales goal of this advertisement
was to identify high principles, high ideals, and high standards
of chemical purity with the name of Squibb. "The Priceless
Ingredient." Pronounce the phrase aloud. Then you hear, without a graph, that price and gred are the two most prominent
syllables. Your ear may also notice that they are surrounded by
less prominent syllables: "The price—less . . . in—gred—i—ent."

Figure 25 is the dynamic or power-time graph of this phrase
. . . with these phonetic values: Thə prīs lĭs ĭn greed dĭ ĕnt. The
d is shared between two syllables. The writer might observe that
if prīs—lĭs were pronounced prīs—lĕs, the change in the second
syllable would hardly affect the power pattern at all. If speech
were extremely rapid, and lĭs or lĕs were pronounced ləs," the
same general power rhythm would appear . . . but the prominence of prīs would be increased. The word ĭn—greed—dĭ—
ĕnt might be slurred or swiftly pronounced so that the short
vowels ĭ and ĕ made the weak, grunty little ə sound. But in this
case, too, the prominence of the most powerful syllable greed
would only become more conspicuous, and the pattern more
clear-cut.

Figure 25 shows that the regularity in the rise and fall of the

© 1958 O. M. C. C. Courtesy of E. R. Squibb and Sons,
Division of Olin Mathieson Chemical Corporation.

Figure 24

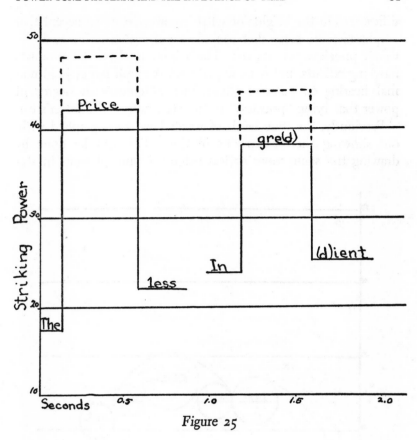

Figure 25

syllables gives some balance of syllabic power. The balance in
the vocal rhythm we can easily hear without a graph. But the
diagram portrays details that the mind's ear may not perceive.
It reveals that extra precision of emphasis, that slightly higher
striking power, which makes "the priceless" sound more prominent to the ear than "ingredient." Compare your enunciation
of the key sounds in the phrase: "The priceless . . . ingredient."
Notice how you hear the power differences between the syllables
of "The priceless" more distinctly than between the syllables
in "ingredient." The graph depicts these finer distinctions. The

differences in the heights of syllabic power create an accent that
emphasizes the story that the advertiser wishes to be told. He
wants pricelessness stressed. The reason is clear. All products
have ingredients, but few are priceless. A graph has assisted normal hearing to perceive those finer differences in degree of
power that bring "priceless" to the attention of the buyer's ear.

Previously, the tone levels of words have been graphed without showing their extensions in time. This can be done by
drawing the same more or less extended time plateaus in sec-

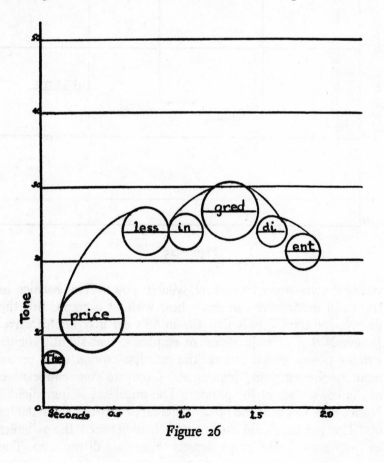

Figure 26

onds that already have been used to present the striking power
of words on dynamic graphs. Then, taking half the length of
the duration plateaus as radii, encompass each plateau or time
line with a circle. The resultant circles will be larger for long-
durational words or syllables and smaller for short ones.

Figure 26 is a tone-time diagram of "The priceless ingredient."

The reader might observe that the graph, Figure 26, is drawn on
the same scale, running from 0 to 50, which portrays dynamic

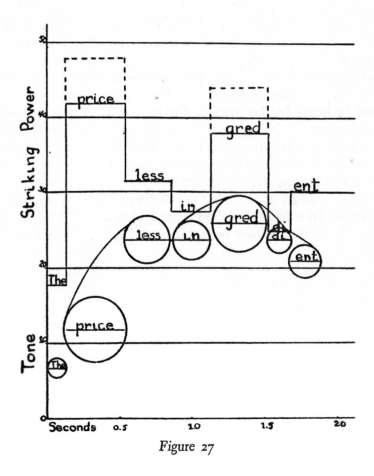

Figure 27

patterns. Because tone levels possess numbers that run from 2 to 26 and because striking power plateaus (excepting weak words such as *to, the, a, of,* and weak syllables such as *bl, en, ly*) have altitude numbers that rise from 26 to 50, the patterns of tone and power rarely overlap. The tone levels are almost always below the power levels. Their horizontal time extensions in seconds are identical. Therefore, it is possible to draw power-time and tonal-time patterns on the same graph—one above the other—with a simultaneous and clearly distinct presentation of each pattern in complete detail. The space and time savings are obvious. Figure 27 is such a diagram of "The priceless ingredient."

When the reader inspects the patterns of Figure 27, his first observation might be the fact that the dynamic curve is the one that he hears. In this instance the tone pattern lacks auditory fidelity. But this is not always the case. In some forms of writing the tone pattern is the one we hear. The following chapter discusses in detail the relative audibility of tone and dynamic patterns and presents the conditions that determine our hearing of these two kinds of rhythms. For the writer who is interested in making the audibility of his language become clear to readers or listeners, the information in the next chapter is important.

8

Hearing Tone and Power Patterns

THE MIND'S EAR PERPETUALLY DETECTS, DISCRIMINATES, AND perceives patterns of intensity or tone whenever the air moves in winds and whispers, in speech or music, in cries, chimes, storms, in the waves of seas, or in the murmurs and pulse of cities. Monotones or unvarying intensities will not stimulate keen impressions. The brain organizes its auditory patterns by hearing differences in intensity and changes in tone. The intensities are produced by pressures on the ear drum, the tones by sympathetic vibrations of the nerves and materials in the inner ear. Although changes in intensity and tone modify each other's effects on hearing, and although their impressions vary with their durations, they bombard the ear as if they were competitors seeking to gain access to the channels of the mind. The brain constantly shifts its attention from one to the other. It makes auditory compromises. *Occasionally the patterns are similar in shape and approximate the congruence of geometric figures. Then the sound patterns are clearest.* The effects of tonality and intensity reinforce each other. The nature of the sounds at the source and the influence of habit will determine which kind of auditory pattern, and how much of it, will dominate the brain.

Figure 28 is a comparison of a tone diagram with a dynamic graph of the first line in "Humpty Dumpty sat on a wall" that

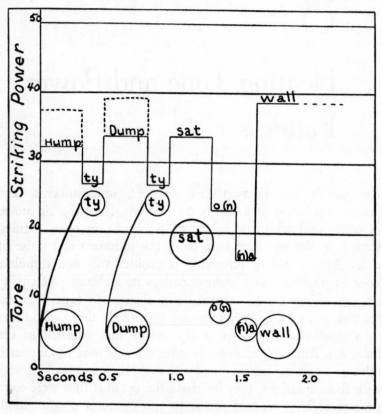

Figure 28

illustrates how basic dimensions of sound affect our auditory intelligence.

The writer should read carefully the dynamic and the tone patterns of Figure 28. Then he should ask himself this question:

"When I say, in a natural manner, 'Humpty Dumpty sat on a wall,' which of the two rhythms do I hear most clearly, the tone pattern or the dynamic one?" After the line has been spoken aloud several times there will be no doubt in the reader's mind that the power rhythm dominates the channels of hearing and captures the attention of his brain.

Why does our mind prefer to pay attention to a rise in the power of a stream of words when their tone falls, or to a drop in syllabic power while the tone is swinging up high?

From 50 to 95 per cent of the striking power of words resides in their vowels. This sizable percentage variation occurs because consonants contribute striking power to words and words may contain anywhere from no consonants to five of them. Despite these fluctuations, the influence of vowel power is a major factor in the striking powers of syllables and words.

Our judgments of the loudness of vowel tones are involved with the ear's interpretation of what constitutes the conspicuousness or acoustic prominence of a vowel sound. To make these judgments some auditory training is required. A vowel's attention-getting characteristics, like other tones, partly depends on variations in the sensitivity of hearing to different frequency levels. They also depend on the time duration and the intensity of their most resonated tone. These remarks should make the writer realize that evaluating the striking powers of vowels is not simple.

When we appreciate fully what we mean by the tone of a vowel, it is not surprising that the levels of vowel tones do not ascend in the same order as their striking powers. The tone of a vowel is the apparent center of all its resonated frequency regions. It is that . . . and nothing more. The level of each vowel's tone is the altitude of its position on a scale that runs from low to high. That is the meaning of the tone levels of vowels which, when calibrated, determine the tone numbers of words or syllables. Striking power numbers, by contrast, were developed from an entirely different experimental interest. Here the objective was to estimate the capacity of each vowel to capture the listener's attention. The average time extension, decibel loss between normal speech and the threshold of hearing, and auditory sensitivity to frequency levels each contributed to the construction called "striking power." The purpose of this construction is to express with numbers a vowel's conspicuousness to the ear—its ability to attract attention. The validity of the striking power numbers were checked by hearing tests, tests that in the final analysis were decisive.

Naturally, it is common sense to expect that vowel numbers that were intentionally evolved to reveal the auditory prominence of vowels will produce patterns that command our attention in preference to dissimilar patterns of the tone levels of vowels. This means that a reader of a dynamic rhythm and a tone rhythm of the same words will hear the former in preference to the latter whenever the two simultaneously move in opposite directions. The reader can judge for himself whether his hearing chooses to follow the power or the dissimilar tone rhythm on the graph of "Humpty Dumpty sat on a wall." If most readers do not select the power pattern, then the striking-power numbers in this book are wrong.

Although vowels account for the larger part of the vocal energy in words, the contributions of consonants and semivowels are by no means negligible. Whatever they do contribute tends to feature the contours of striking power patterns at the expense of the tonal audibility of words. The reason is that consonants are noises, not tones. Semivowels also possess noise characteristics. Their overtone structure is less fixed, less clear, and therefore lacks the decisiveness that we hear in vowel tones. The phonation of semivowel and consonantal power supplies from zero to 45 per cent of the striking power of words. Single-vowel words such as I, a, you account for the zero per cent. Consonants and semivowels account for almost 45 per cent of the striking

power in words like *drenched, grill, brooms*. At least one consonant or semivowel occurs in over 50 per cent of the most
frequently spoken words. Therefore an author *must* write these
noises into most of his script. He cannot rule consonants out
of existence. He cannot disregard them as a singer who intensi-
fies the overtones of vowels three hundred times with vocal
power throbbing out of the lungs and the vibrant vocal chords
(the reason why sung words sometimes lose intelligibility). All
spoken language is studded with hisses, percussions, and oral
hums.

The result can be summarized: *over 90 per cent of words beat
the drum of the ear with the intensity of noisy consonants and
semivowels whose loudness produces from 10 to 45 per cent of
the striking power of syllables and words. Because the effect of
these sounds is not tonal they convey little of the sensation we
hear in the rising and falling tone rhythms founded on the vowel
scale.* This characteristic of speech is the second factor that
makes a striking power pattern among words dominate the mind
when it differs in shape from the pattern of their tones.

The writer is in the position of a composer who works with
a very special seventy-five-piece orchestra that lends itself to
unique principles of composition. Twenty-two of the instruments in this orchestra are noise or percussion devices such as
drums, cymbals, tambourines, castanets, gongs, triangles,
whistles, friction-timbred klaxons, and whips. Another group of
twenty-two instruments are bellows with overtones that hum
and roar in short intervals of time. Thirty tuned-up tonal pieces
made of strings, horns, and reeds make up the rest of the orchestra. Each of these instruments will play only one note on
the scale. Their fundamentals are approximately the same. So
is the number of their overtones.

The principles of composition imposed by this strange as-
semblage of noise gadgets and tone-making devices are several.
Ninety per cent of the measures must have at least one note

produced by either a noise piece or one of the bellows. Fifty per cent must contain at least two such notes. Only one measure out of ten can be made up solely with the purely tonal note of the wood-wind, stringed, or brass instruments. The duration of a strictly tonal measure is less than half of the average one. There is still another restriction. Between 10 and 45 per cent of the power of each measure of music must be manufactured by percussions, hisses, hums, and roars. This imaginary orchestra and its problems presents the situation that confronts the writer, the director, and the composer with the orchestra of the language.

What effects can this orchestra and these principles of composition create? It can beat rhythms dependent on noise rather than tone, percussion rhythms dynamic and clear. The patterns this music taps or pounds are closer to primitive than to modern orchestral music. In this music the slurred syllable, rather than the note, is the source of accent.

The composer would have to learn the effects of combining specific noise and bellows instruments with his limited number of tones. He is restricted to playing many of his tones with the same loudness. Since only one tone can be played at a time, he cannot produce chords or harmonic relationships. His main source of melody is rhythm. Only tone or power patterns and the accents of timbre are at the disposal of the composer.

These patterns may be used for four different effects:

First, his tone and his power rhythms can run in opposite directions and be different in shape. For the reasons discussed previously, the dynamic power rhythms will then dominate the mind's ear.

Second, he can make his two kinds of rhythms assume a similar structure and move in the same direction; then their effects will reinforce each other, and the brain will not be compelled to divide its attention between them. This gives the most striking and clearest auditory effects.

Third, he can maintain his dynamic pattern on an unchanging and constant level while the tone rhythm varies. In this case the only possible auditory discrimination is tonal. To achieve this effect it is necessary to build syllables or words with consistent differences in striking power throughout phrases or sentences. Naturally, the technique of adjusting the power values of specific syllables and words must be carried out by the writer.

40   42   42   34 33 33   37

The green-grown grain of the wind-sown seeds on the West's

41   41

broad plains

is a sentence devised to illustrate this relationship. The almost similar striking power numbers appear over the prominent words. The reader can easily hear the tone pattern. When the same tone rhythm is carried by words with a more varied power structure it becomes less clear.

29 16 27   30.5 30   37   34.5 27.5 40

The timothy in the heat-stirred winds on the western lands

is a sentence that lacks the tonal clarity of *The green-grown grain of the wind-sown seeds on the West's broad plains.* The similarity in the power patterns of *timothy* and *western lands* and the repetition of the connective phrases *in the, on the* allows the ear to perceive some faint tone in the phrase. However, the same tone pattern that appears again in the following sentence is not heard at all.

38   34 29.5   31.5 30.5 38   34.5 27.5

The reaped mown hay in the yellow stacks on the western

38

fields

What rhythm we do hear is caused by the consistent positions of the short, weak words, *in the* and *on the.* It is dynamic in quality, not tonal.

Fourth, the writer can keep a tone rhythm constant while he varies the flow of word power. In this case the mind's attention has so few adjustments to make on one level of hearing and feeling that it requires little energy or effort to focus simultaneously on a different auditory pattern. The radio announcement

$$34.5 \quad 31.5 \quad 34.5 \quad 31.5 \quad 34.5 \quad 31.5$$
Smoke Kools, smoke Kools, smoke Kools

has this pattern relationship. The brain associates a cold feeling with the low monotone of the vowels and enjoys their melodious overtones at the same time that it listens to the dynamic rhythm of the words. The power is medium high, somewhat flat, and prolonged in time. This phrase suggests the techniques for clarifying tones. Repeat them, and stabilize their consonantal environment. Rhyme is one way to attain this effect. A subtler process is to combine consonants and semivowels whose tone-influence levels occupy the same position on the vowel scale as the vowels with which they are joined. The tones of *schist, stitch, yeast, scene, need* are slightly higher and keener than the tones of *will, rib, beer, leave, meal.*

In the following verse,

Humpty Dumpty sat on a wall
Humpty Dumpty had a great fall

there is an example of the second relationship between tone and power patterns. It is the phrase, *had a great fall,* whose tone and striking power rhythms both move in the same direction and have a similar shape. This phrase gives the only touch of feeling in the verse. Figure 29 is the graph of its tone and dynamic rhythms.

The reinforcement of the tone and dynamic curves makes the rhythm of "had a great fall" quite clear. If the reader will recite "Humpty Dumpty had a GREAT fall" in the dramatic way that children do when they stress *great,* he will notice a sound

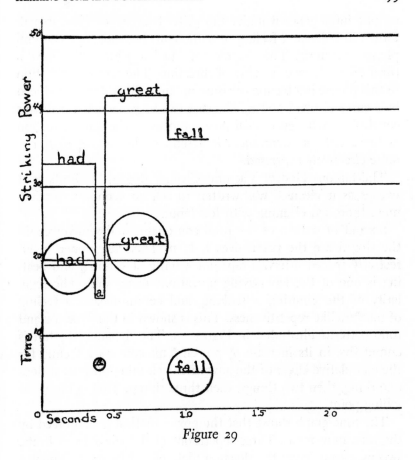

Figure 29

track is being drawn across his imagination that swings up and then descends from a height. The path of this sound track flashes a phonetic signal. First, it conveys a sense of a rise appropriate to the looming up of a wall. Then it drops down in a manner fitting to Humpty Dumpty's fall. A sound image has expressed the feeling of the action that the words refer to.

We previously saw on a graph of the dynamic rhythm flowing through *The priceless ingredient* (Fig. 27) that audio-scriptic intelligence will give the writer two effects. First, its patterns can balance a feeling or a thought. Second, they can emphasize meaning. The diagram of "had a great fall" shows a third effect. It gives a sense of direction. The sense of direction in this phrase is a feeling of rising up and falling down produced by a curve of word power. The case can be generalized with this conclusion: *whenever vocal power moves in the same direction as the events or occurrences it describes, the subject matter is more effectively expressed.*

The famous Hoover Vacuum Cleaner slogan, "It beats as it sweeps as it cleans," was written to sell an economic service: more thorough cleaning with less labor.

Six out of sixteen of the total consonants and semivowels in the slogan are the percussives *t, k, p*. Their recurrence in effectively spaced intervals taps out a sense of beating; and beating is one of the laborsaving operations being sold. The regularity of the phrasing is striking, and communicates a feeling of machinelike repetitiveness. This is shown in the dynamic and tone patterns illustrated in Figure 30. The dynamic rhythm is cumulative in its increase of power. This conveys a feeling for the cumulative effect of the advertiser's cleaning process: it does one thing, then two things, then three things. That is the main selling point.

The tone graph shows that the power rhythm is reinforced by the tone movement. Three repetitions of the vowel *ee* in beats, sweeps, cleans, gives the slogan a high, clear tone that simulates an echo. The repetitive echo expresses "it beats." A high, clear tone tends to be associated with brightness. Brightness and clarity are the ultimate purposes of good cleaning. The tone pattern, besides its rhythmic contribution, gives to the sales appeal an emotional aura that fits the service being sold: efficient cleaning.

The diagram shown in Figure 30 demonstrates again that when a striking power and a tone rhythm slope in the same direction and have the same shape, their sounds are clearest and

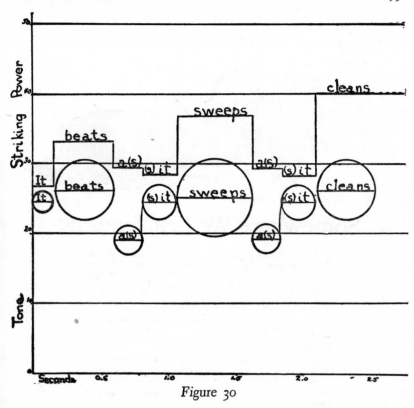

Figure 30

their effects most precise. It illustrates another effect of phonetic intelligence: that of cumulative power. An accumulative
change in word power may increase or decrease in the manner
of Figure 31.

INCREASE   DECREASE

Figure 31

Somewhere West of Laramie

SOMEWHERE west of Laramie there's a broncho-busting, steer-roping girl who knows what I'm talking about. She can tell what a sassy pony, that's a cross between greased lightning and the place where it hits, can do with eleven hundred pounds of steel and action when he's going high, wide and handsome.

The truth is—the Playboy was built for her.

Built for the lass whose face is brown with the sun when the day is done of revel and romp and race.

She loves the cross of the wild and the tame.

There's a savor of links about that car—of laughter and lilt and light—a hint of old loves—and saddle and quirt. It's a brawny thing—yet a graceful thing for the sweep o' the Avenue.

Step into the Playboy when the hour grows dull with things gone dead and stale.

Then start for the land of real living with the spirit of the lass who rides, lean and rangy, into the red horizon of a Wyoming twilight.

JORDAN MOTOR CAR COMPANY, Inc., Cleveland, Ohio

Figure 32

Accumulative forms give to fluctuations of word power a sense of direction that is more sustained and definite than a single fluctuation. Dynamic patterns have now produced four effects:

A rhythmic balance of a feeling or idea.
Emphasis of meaning.
A sense of direction.
A cumulative increase or decrease in power.

The successful advertisement that appears in Figure 32 aims to associate certain emotions with the Jordan car. They are emotions of the open west, with a spirit of daring, youth, and the carefree. They have a sweep to them that swings along easily, gracefully, as they celebrate a conquest of space. The essence of this feeling is contained in the headline of the copy, "Somewhere West of Laramie," whose tone and dynamic graphs are presented in Figure 33.

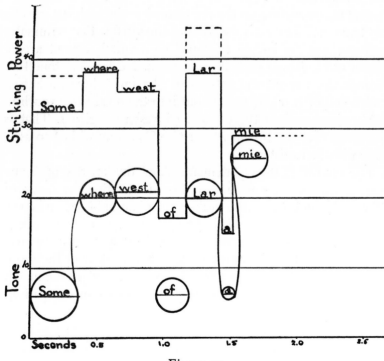

Figure 33

The dynamic and tonal patterns of most of the syllables on the diagram of Figure 33 are similar and reinforce each other. Yet the over-all effect of "Somewhere West of Laramie" is tonal rather than dynamic. The predominance of the tone rhythm in "Somewhere West of Laramie" depends on several factors. One of them is the repetition of the vowels ŭ, ĕ, ĕ, ŭ, ĕ, ŭ in the words and successive syllables some, where, west, of, Lar, a. The internal rhyme of "where" and "Lar" is particularly effective because the tone levels of w and r have the same height on the vowel scale. The rhyme anchors the tone pattern and makes it more definite. The regular up-and-down gallop of the melodious rhythm catches the equestrian spirit of the ease, the swing, and the grace that the motor car company wished to identify with the Jordan roadster. The finest touch in the tone effect is the ending of the rhythm on the rise of tone in the high last syllable of "Laramie." The extra duration of the syllable that terminates a phrase and the ending of "mie" on a vowel without a consonant or semivowel gives it an unstopped, extra clear tone that ascends. As a result the pattern of "Laramie" leaves a lasting impression of swinging up and out into the open like a youthful driver speeding into the expanse of western horizons. That is the mood that the Jordan Motor Car Company wished to associate with its roadster.

The validity of these statements about the key role of "Laramie" in this phrase can be proved by substituting the names of other cities and testing the evaluations of an unbiased audience. This experiment was carried out with a group of four college graduates, two of whom were born and brought up in France. To familiarize them with the purpose and context of the headline, they were shown the entire ad. Then they judged the merits of Chicago, Milwaukee, Helena, and Santa Fe in comparison with Laramie. Here are their evaluations.

All four agreed, without hesitation, that Chicago and Milwaukee were bad substitutes. This can be verified by the reader:

"Somewhere West of Laramie," "Somewhere West of Chicago," "Somewhere West of Milwaukee." The headline "Somewhere West of Helena" was considered more effective than "Somewhere West of Chicago" and "Somewhere West of Milwaukee," but not equal to "Somewhere West of Laramie." Three of the group were unanimous in their judgments that "Somewhere West of Santa Fe" was almost as effective as "Somewhere West of Laramie." One person preferred "Somewhere West of Santa Fe." See Figure 34 on page 100.

Figure 34 is a graph of the names substituted whose patterns in every case substantiate the evaluations of the test group.

The similarity of the tone and dynamic curves of Santa Fe and Laramie can be seen at a glance. Although the first two syllables of Helena are satisfactory, the last syllable drops weakly in power and tone. This destroys the desired effect. The patterns of Chicago obviously demolish the rhythm and the effect. The tone pattern of Milwaukee is satisfactory, but the dynamic pattern runs in opposite directions and is quite different in shape. It completely destroys the rhythm and the effect.

The skeptical reader who doubts the graph's fidelity to large areas of our hearing may notice that these tests are verifications. Scores of other tests gave the same results.

Another factor that features the tonal pattern in "Somewhere West of Laramie" at the expense of the dynamic pattern will be serviceable to the writer who wishes to understand more fully the basis for his clearest effects. It can be summarized: *Whenever a phrase or sentence contains a power and tone pattern that are similar in shape and direction, the pattern whose syllables or verbal levels are separated by wider distances is the pattern that the mind will be most likely to hear and follow.*

Reference to the graph of this headline, Figure 33, shows in detail how much greater are the distances that separate the tone levels of syllables than are the distances between successive plateaus of syllabic power. The reader has observed that the

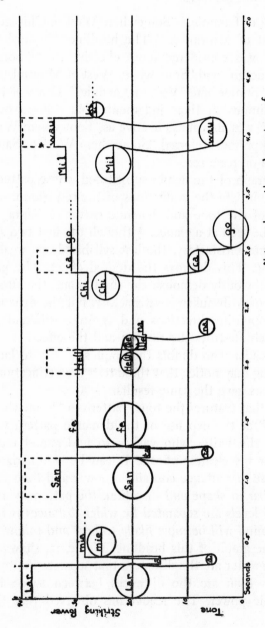

'Milwauki' run in the opposite direction to its tone in contrast to 'Laramie.'

Figure 34

Notice how the dynamics of "Milwauki" run in opposite direction to its tone, in contrast to "Laramie." See also Figure 33, page 97.

tone and dynamic patterns of the words in "It beats as it sweeps
as it cleans," although different in form from "Somewhere West
of Laramie," are also approximately similar in shape and direction. Yet the rhythm of "It beats as it sweeps as it cleans" is
chiefly a power pattern. Evaluation of its graph in Figure 30 reveals that the differences between power plateaus are greater
than between tone levels. Possibly, when the more widely separated nerve endings in the inner ear are affected they send clearer
signals to the brain. The comparative clarity of tone and dynamic
patterns on the basis of distances between the levels of their
syllables can be considered, less theoretically, as a question of
contrast. We do not hear as much tonal distinction in *keen tin*,
keen tin, keen tin, as we do in *keen tune, keen tune, keen tune*.
A name such as *Jane Luke* has a more distinguishable tone variation than *Joan Luke*. The rhythm of *Humpity Dumpity* is dy-
namically clearer than *Humpty Dumpty*. These comparative effects are analogous to discriminating more clearly a color design
that contrasts red against green or blue against orange than
brown next to red or blue against green. Although the achievement of contrast in phonetic patterns is complicated by several
factors, its effectiveness warrants a writer's serious consideration.

One of the many impressive tonal lines in Samuel Taylor
Coleridge's "Rime of the Ancient Mariner" is "Alone, alone,
all, all alone;/Alone on a wide, wide sea." This line is an instance
of constant tone and varying dynamics. But the dynamic plateaus are separated by such extremely short time intervals that
our hearing blends them into a single flat plateau of apparent
power. The result is monotonous, except at the end of the line
where the tones of "wide, wide sea" rise. Figure 35 is a graph
illustrating these facts. For purposes of comparison the lower
section of the graph presents the tone pattern of "Somewhere
West of Laramie."

The general feeling induced by "Alone, alone, all, all
alone;/Alone on a wide, wide sea" is as monotonous and melan-

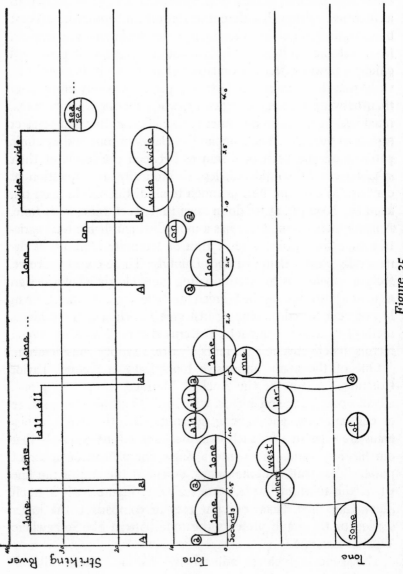

Figure 35

choly as a litany of groans. The constancy of the low, unbroken level of tone is due to the low vowels and the resonating of their lower overtones by numerous *l*'s. This is a fitting accompaniment to the sorrow and terror in the ancient mariner's agony and guilt. In contrast, the singsong galloping of the tone rhythm in "Somewhere West of Laramie" is gay. The over-all patterns in these two lines shade the meaning of their somewhat similar tonal endings. The tone rhythm in each case swings up to a high-level syllable unstopped by a consonant, and both end on a note suggesting a sense of opening, expanding vistas. But their dynamics differ. The power and tone patterns of "wide, wide sea" run in opposite directions, while the tones of the terminal word in "Somewhere West of Laramie" are sustained by their dynamic pattern (Fig. 33). The rising tone of "wide, wide sea" and the open oral upsweep of the two *w*'s are descriptive rather than emotional. In this context they help us to sense the solitary ancient mariner on his fantastic ship gazing out at the vast sea's expanse. The impressions of the last three sounds in the pattern of each line depend on the larger tone patterns in which they appear and on the context of the entire piece of writing. These analyses show that it is unwise to isolate an effect without regard for both its over-all phonetic patterns and the message of the subject matter.

The phonetic patterns of the phrases and sentences discussed in this chapter last from one and a half to three seconds. They are carried by the sounds of groups of words, not by a single syllable or a monosyllabic word whose time duration extends, roughly, one tenth as long. The signals that these phonetic patterns flash to the reader-listener are not completely dependent on the accepted meanings of words. Once organized, they develop acoustic and auditory characteristics peculiar to themselves. That is why they are able to communicate some effects and feelings that the scrambled, deadened sounds and the trite references of conventionally used words cannot express. These sound images give the writer additional dimensions—the dimensions of sound—to cope with subject matter whose scope and diversity of feeling tax the signaling power in the customary meanings of words.

The auditory effects that result from the four possible orientations of simultaneous tone and dynamic patterns are the most abstract forms of audio-scriptic intelligence. The same principles of analysis and composition can be applied to all languages with the possible exception of those that rely heavily on pitch inflection for their meaning, such as Chinese. Because the people in a country produce their own speech and, in time, alter the characteristics of their national language, the fidelity of conversational tones and power values will be lost after a few centuries. But the auditory intelligibility created by the orientations of parallel phonetic patterns will endure as long as the human nervous system and brain. They are keys to the music in man's speech.

9

In the Light of Auditory Intelligence

THE PIONEER AMONG JINGLES WAS THE PEPSI-COLA JINGLE. IT IS unusually interesting because it was sensationally successful. For the writer this jingle has a special interest: its effectiveness was due more to clever writing than to theatrical fireworks. The super-catchy melody, the sexy voice, the sound effects made by gadgets, and all the other artifices of showmanship played minor roles in the success of the jingle. The spice in the lure was the phonetic intelligence of the copy.

The emotional appeal of this jingle is "pep," and here is a good example of the power of an effective brand name: "Pepsi-Cola." The public's attention had been aroused and stimulated for years by lawsuits against the Coca-Cola Corporation over the alleged narcotic affect of coca leaf extracts. Was the coca extract in Coca-Cola habit-forming and injurious? That was the highly publicized question. The press had built up an image in the public's mind that identified Coca-Cola with some mysterious ingredient, akin to cocaine or opium, that possessed a marvelous mental kick. The drink became endowed with the spirit of a strange, forbidden fruit that would invigorate. Those who wrote the "pep" into Pepsi-Cola were not exactly naïve in their strategy to capture the syrup market from the Coca-Cola Corporation.

> Pepsi-Cola hits the spot,
> Two full glasses, that's a lot.
> Twice as much for a nickel, too,
> Pepsi-Cola is the drink for you.

Now, "pep" is a healthy emotion, an American state of mind, a home-cooked product as familiar as corn on the cob or apple pie. It suggests eager beaver boy scouts or baseball players running around the diamond, not the cocaine dreams of shifty-eyed snowballs. "Pep" is full of speed, liveliness, lift, brightness, nimbleness, bounce, and sharpness touched with strength.

The economic message in the jingle is: buy more Cola for less money. How do the sounds of speech and their patterns build up an effect of peppiness, and convince the radio listener that Pepsi-Cola is a good buy?

The first line of this jingle, the most important line in any jingle, is loaded with the sharp, quick percussive consonants *k, t,* and *p.* The staccato effect is striking, and is filled with the liveliness, the lift and skippiness we associate with pep. On the basis of the average number of occurrences of *k, t,* and *p* in normal telephone conversations we can make a percentage comparison of the frequency with which *k, t* and *p* occur in the first line of the jingle. It amounts to 38 per cent more than the average. That is a striking surplus. The staccato quality of these percussives contribute that touch of strength and sharpness that is so much a part of the feeling of peppiness.

Nor do these explosively rapid consonants crowd just the first line. They sound through all the lines of the jingle, and, along with the percussive *ch,* appear 14 per cent more frequently than they do in average speech. The copy is sprinkled with nimble little ticking sounds suggesting the nimbleness and deftness of "pep."

The effect of peppiness is also conveyed by the vowels. The vowels are the speedy ones that skip along in tiny periods of time such as ĕ in *Pepsi*, ə in *a*, ĭ in *hits*, and o͞o in *full*. Pronounce them aloud. You will hear their swiftness. There are 20 per cent more of these rapid vowels in the Pepsi-Cola jingle than are present in normal speech. A 20 per cent difference is quite a surplus.

The combination of speedy vowels and consonants shortens the average time of the syllables in the jingle by 0.05 seconds. The total effect is to put speed in the language and suggest that sense of being alert and quick that we experience when we say: "We feel peppy." The swift vowels and consonants that contribute to this feeling are marked on the power-time graph of Figure 36 by arrows.

When you look at this graph, observe how the brand name, Pepsi-Cola, concentrates in itself percussive consonants and quick vowels that the jingle expands and develops. Since brand names depend on speech over the radio and video for their publicity, the contribution of auditory intelligence for the naming of a product is obvious.

The clicking consonants and the transient vowels, which do not give the ear enough time to hear full clear tones, make the lines dynamic. Their tone values do not command attention. Hence, the tone graph is omitted.

The previous graph shows that certain words are prominent and high. They are: *glass, twice, drink,* and to a lesser extent *that's, much, lot,* and *spot.* These words are charged with power. They arise out of their environment of unaccented syllables to strike our ear with a maximum impact. The force of the impact is partly due to the dramatic contrast between the low energy level of an unusual number of weak syllables and the high power levels of *twice, glass,* and *drink.* There are other words with more intrinsic power, but few can highlight their power against a background of so many feeble syllables. The jumping up of these

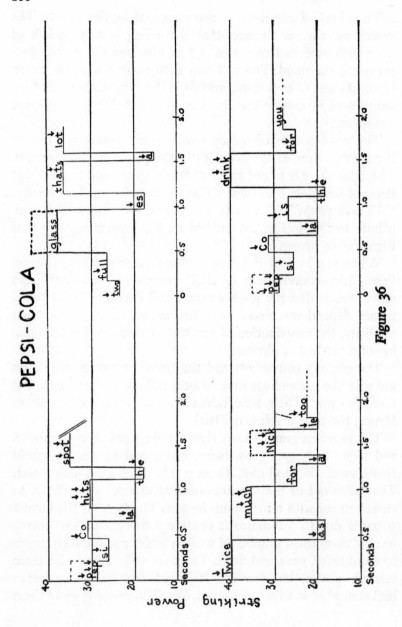

Figure 36

peaks of vocal power gives us a feeling of the bounce and the lift in the lively emotion of peppiness.

"Glass—that's—lot—twice—much—drink," the striking words that ring in our ears, do more than advertise pep. They shout the economic argument: more Cola for less money. This service of phonetic intelligence is as valuable as the expression of pep.

The shape of the curve of the phrase, "two full glasses," as it appears on the graph, has a tallness and a fullness that supports the economic message: a big volume for a little nickel. Notice how the power curve of "nickel, too" drops down to a low loudness level and suggests, graphically, the story it is trying to tell: a nickel is a little. These illustrations of the communicative powers in the acoustic shapes of whole phrases are additional examples of the conception of audio-scriptic intelligence applied throughout this book. When either the shape or the direction of a phonetic curve is similar to the shape of a writer's subject matter or to the direction in which it moves, then the phonetic pattern reinforces and expresses the meaning of the subject matter. It helps to tell the writer's story and acts like the shaking of the head with saying "No," or the shrugging of the shoulders to toss off responsibility in saying "I don't know." It is a phonetic gesture.

If we examine closely the power and tone patterns in the famous elegiac line by Walt Whitman, "When lilacs last in the door-yard bloomed," it becomes apparent that the power pattern dominates. That is what our ear perceives. There are tonal effects, but they are slight. The diagram in Figure 37 shows which syllables and words we naturally accent. When we scan the patterns, we naturally hear more emphasis given to the first syllable in *lilacs* (*li*lacs) than to *when*. The power syllable is favored. Likewise, we do not stress the high tone level of the word *in*. Its somewhat weak power level is heard as it would be spoken, i.e., without accent. Certainly we would not give more auditory or phonetic prominence to the swift little word *the*

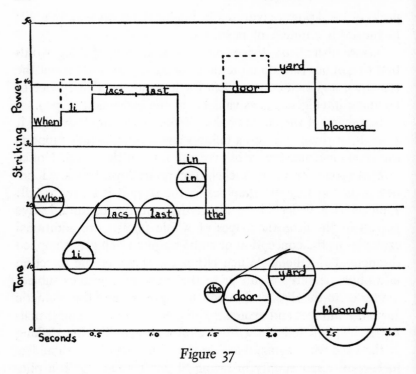

Figure 37

than to the powerful word *door*. Consequently, the tonal track between *the* and *door* is not followed. Again, we see how the ear follows the paths of power in preference to tone when contradictory directions in the two curves compel a choice. The pattern details in the graph permit the reader to test the relative audibility of these rhythms by reading them silently, then aloud.

The line has an extra decisive rhythm because of its timbre. The tongue lifts of *w* and *l* that occur when they swing and blend into the high-toned vowels give a lilt to every syllable in "When lilacs last." Because the *lă* in *last* repeats the *lă* in *lilacs* it acquires some tonal audibility. And "door-yard bloomed" with similar tone-dynamic directions of the syllables, and low-toned vowels in every syllable, do give the ear a tonal impression. Accordingly, we can conclude: "When lilacs last in the door-yard bloomed" is a dynamic-timbre line with audible tones in some segments of it. If we intentionally alter the word order of this line by writing it "When lilacs bloomed last in the door-yard," the rhythm, the poetry, the timbre lift, and the feelings carried by them are all gone. Gone, too, is the melancholy innuendo of ending the line on the depressed level of a low tone whose time duration is drawn out long, i.e., the word *bloomed.* A prosaic statement has displaced the language of poetry and mood.

This treatment shows how delicately and perpetually the ear distributes its attention among the tone, timbre, power, and time of syllables and words. It also demonstrates how sensitive the effectiveness of a phonetic rhythm can be to the most minute change in detail. That is why good poetry is rare. And that is why auditory discipline is a skill required by every author who wishes to write fully effective prose.

Up to here we have presented no dynamic or tonal diagram to show the effects of these phonetic techniques on public speech.

In Figure 38 are graphed the opening words of the Gettysburg address. On the same graph appears an alternate beginning to Lincoln's speech. *"Eighty*-seven years ago" is substituted for *"Four score and* seven years ago," alternate words underlined. Both statements say exactly the same thing. Their only difference is their phonetic patterns. "Four score and" starts off the address with more rhetorical sonorousness and far more attention-getting power; the vowels in *four* and *score* contribute a repetitive tone that develops an echo in sequent words that contain the same vowel tone, i.e., *"Four score—forefathers brought forth"* (identical tones underlined). These effects are lost when the sharp, weak, shrill "eighty-seven" begins the address. Furthermore, the graph shows that Lincoln's "Four score and . . ." expression is longer in time (2.4 seconds without interword pauses) compared to 1.7 seconds for the quick little

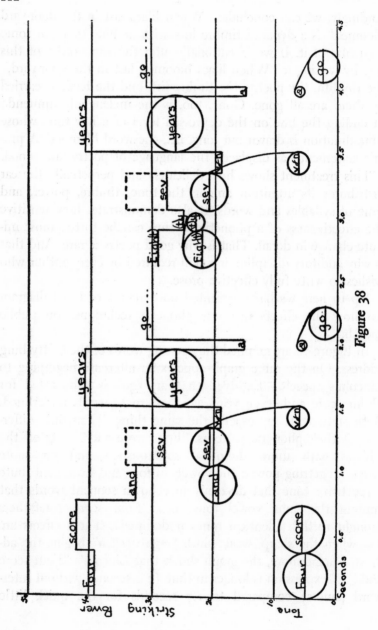

Figure 38

"Eighty-seven. . . ." The longer-lasting opening words permit the ear to catch more completely that sense of duration which Lincoln wished to associate with the history of the Republic. It may also be seen that the distances between plateaus of tones are greater and more conducive to audibility in Lincoln's words than in the substitute. We observe in this quotation, as in other examples of memorable speech, that auditory judgment was exercised in the composition of the script.

On May 13, 1940, Winston Churchill addressed Parliament as Britain's World War II Prime Minister. This was his famous speech of accession to office that for the first time offered "nothing but blood, toil, tears, and sweat." During the next two and a half years this offer was repeated on five different occasions with some variation in the word order of *Blood, Toil, Sweat, Tears.* Yet, when Mr. Churchill decided to publish his history of this climactic period he chose to title his book *Blood, Sweat, and Tears.*

Eighteen years later the author put this question to two librarians in the New York City 42nd St. library, three librarians of *The New York Times* information bureaus, five mature school teachers, one British clerk (female), three University Press readers, two book editors, and one advertising agency chief copywriter: "How did Churchill complete his famous statement: I have nothing to offer but blood . . . etc.?" Every one of these sixteen people gave the same answer without hesitation. "Nothing but blood, sweat, and tears." This is the phrase that stayed in their memories. When the British clerk heard the words of the original speech she indignantly remarked: "I don't believe Mr. Churchill ever spoke such words. He was too fine a speaker."

Let us see if audio-scriptic intelligence can assist us to understand why *nothing but blood, sweat, and tears* is the statement that people cannot forget. So let us compare the effectiveness of the acoustic patterns of "But blood, sweat, and tears" with "But blood, tears, and sweat." These are revealed on the dia-

114

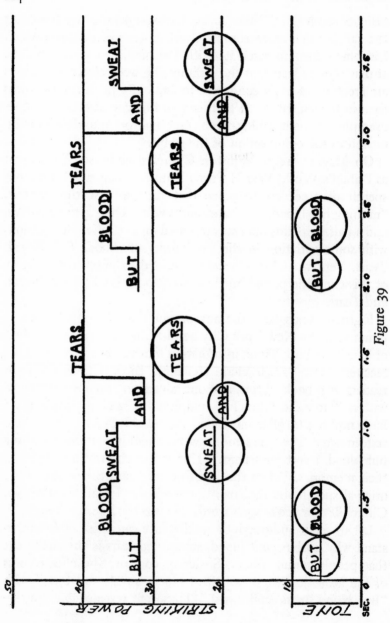

Figure 39

gram of figure 39. There we see that the power and tone patterns of the memorable phrase move in the same direction and therefore reinforce each other's audibility. Not only is the phrase most audible, but the terminal position of *tears*, the most emotionally charged word in the expression, permits the speaker to end the expression on a tonal ring. The crescendo of the phonetic curve enhances the emotion in the meaning of the words. If we move *tears* to the middle of the phrase, the letdown of feeling is shown by the rhythm of the graph.

The simultaneous rise of tone and power is broken; the climactic effect is weakened; and the abrupt, stop-consonant *t* in *sweat* kills the extended duration and the prolonged tone that *tears* holds when it ends the line.

The superior audibility, euphony, and memorability of "blood, sweat and tears!" must have been apparent to Winston Churchill. Otherwise, he would not have featured this order of words as the title of his history.

In passing, it may be observed that this is an example of using written acoustic patterns as a tool of criticism.

These excerpts from speeches reveal that the vibrance of rhetoric does need audio-scriptic intelligence. Why is this true when the phonetic values of these curves are based on mouth or oral phonation rather than on the art of voicing which is so important for the eloquent delivery of speech? There are several reasons. The time rhythms of phrases and sentences are paced by the number of words in groups that start and stop and flow in a succession of periods. Here the average speaking time of words is relevant. So are the probable pauses. Curves of oral power and tone tend to accent an idea. If they do, then their tendency is congenial to the pitch and loudness patterns of a gifted speaker's voice. When oral and throat phonations are in accord they emphasize the meaning of words with two vocal signals. A speaker with a trained voice can intonate "pitch" or "screech" with low-pitched tones. But it is easier for him to make low-pitched tones ring out from such words as "throw" or "growl." It should not be forgotten that the intelligibility of American and English vowels depends on patterns of the most resonated frequency regions in the mouth—not on laryngeal pitch. Similarly, a powerful-voiced orator can make *hit* sound loud. But he can do a better job with *strike*. A good orator deserves a script with rich auditory possibilities.

Thirty years ago, before the Postum Cereal Co. became General Foods, a famous advertisement appeared entitled "Why Men Crack." It sold Postum. Although the intent, the tone, and the policy of this ad belong to a different era, the acoustic patterns of its rhetoric were effective. A few lines from this copy are quoted below.

WHY MEN CRACK

You know them. Strong men, vigorous men, robust men—men who have never had a sick day in their lives. They drive. They drive themselves to the limit. They lash themselves OVER the limit with stimulants. They crack. Often, they crash.

You have seen them afterward. Pitiful shells. The zest gone, the fire gone. Burnt out furnaces of energy. . . .

"FOR EVERY ACTION THERE IS AN EQUAL AND CONTRARY REACTION." You learned the law in physics. It applies to bodies.

For every ounce of energy gained by stimulation . . . physical bankruptcy. Then the crash. . . .

Two million American families avoid caffein by drinking Postum. . . .

The message of this famous advertisement is *The march to destruction to the measure of coffee.* It scolds the reader, warns the reader, and above all, scares the reader. Once the fear of noxious caffein is drilled into the reader's mind, it is a cinch to promote an alleged health-building substitute made of wholesome whole wheat, natural bran, "A little sweetening. Nothing

more." Postum. The copy instills FEAR by sheer weight and ac-
cumulation of description and argument in its step by step story
of *The march to destruction to the measure of coffee.*

That is the emotional appeal, and that is the package, and that
is the raw material for phonetic intelligence to analyze.

The march toward disaster begins with steady, regular steps:
(You know them). (Strong men), (vigorous men), (robust
men). All these phrases in parentheses are short and even in
time. The difference between successive phrases is not more
than 0.07 seconds of speaking time (Fig. 41).

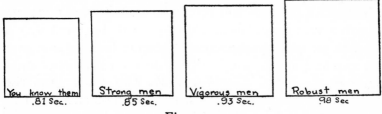

Figure 41

The spacing of these phrases shows the first indication of a
cumulative effect. The inevitability of this progression is pounded
into our ears by repeating the word *men* in "strong men, vigorous men, robust men." *Strong* is a strong word, *robust* is a power
word. Not sissies and weaklings, but the mightiest of the mighty
are marked for destruction. The march continues: (Men who
have never had a sick day in their lives). Again *men* is repeated,
and the mood is resounded, beating into the ear an impression
of many men. The duration of this phrase and the again repeated
echo of men sum up, cumulatively, and again reverberate the
footfalls of the steps toward destruction. It is phonetically accumulative, and its gathering volume of sound suggests the
pyramiding of the toxic effect of day-after-day doses of caffein.
We sense the build-up of a dramatic climax.

Speech duration

*You know them. Strong men, vigorous men,
      robust men,*   3.60 seconds
*Men who have never had a sick day in their
      lives.*   3.24 seconds

The periods of the terse phrases are close to the time limits where duration has its maximum effect on the loudness of speech. The style is a sledgehammer one. The hammering of repeated words is a primitive technique that captures the attention of many, but whose obviousness and loudness offend the few.

The attack proceeds. But before the crackup a few more cups of coffee must be imbibed. Therefore, with the word *lives* in our ears, we return to the repeated beats of the regular steps of the march: (in their lives). (They drive.) (They drive themselves to the limit.) *Lives-drive-drive.* The power curve rises because *drive* is louder than *lives.* The speech duration of "They drive themselves to the limit" is almost four times the amount of "They drive." The pyramiding is multiplied by four. The march goes on (Fig. 42) as the cumulative effect is once again increased: (They lash themselves OVER the limit with stimulants). Now we reach the climax, the crackup! (They crack.) (Often they crash.) *Lash-crack-crash.*

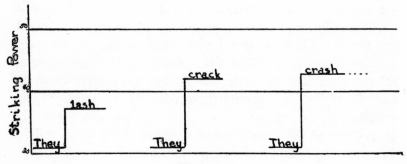

Figure 42

By this time, every hypochondriac in the U.S.A. who reads the copy trembles before the nightmare of measuring out his days and digging up his grave with coffee spoons.

The next paragraph plays on the self-pity of the hypochondriac like a musical chord. The mood is one of regret blended with sympathy. (You have seen them afterwards) . . . (Burnt-out furnaces of energy). Word power runs along evenly. There are no sharp disruptions. The energy plateaus of those phrases are dropped down to flat, low levels whose small voice is the tone of those subdued or broken. There is not one high-powered word or syllable in the graphs of Figures 43 and 44.

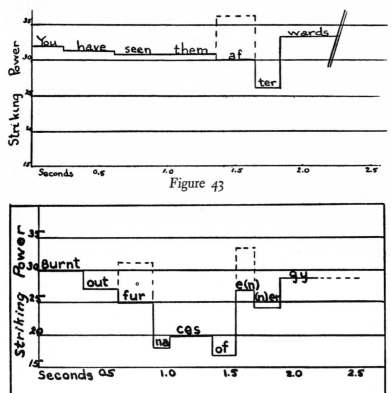

Figure 43

Figure 44

Notice the hollow impression of the pattern of "Burnt-out furnaces of energy" and how the graph expresses a hollow feeling through the shape of the sound track. This phonetic form contributes something to auditory intelligence.

Interspersed among the sentences of sadness in this paragraph of melancholy are the terse statements: (Pitiful shells), (The zest gone), (the fire gone). These intense, short phrases throw back at us an echo of (strong men), (vigorous men), (robust men), and, like sorrow itself, turn our eyes backward in time toward our terrible loss, our loss of the strength leached out of our body—by coffee.

These abrupt, concise phrases of the second paragraph give us the key to the mechanics of the author's style: a continual interruption of ten- to twenty-word sentences with clipped, punch statements of two to three words.

There are other, minor points of phonetic intelligence in the two paragraphs analyzed. The word gone lowers the end of the phrases (the zest gone), (the fire gone) with a dying-down tone (Fig. 45) appropriate to sorrow.

Occasionally, the copy associates tonally the harshness of the fate of coffee drinkers with the blurred strains of vowel dissonance that sound through the phrases: (lash themselves), (crack . . . often).

The phonetic technique of the headline "Why men crack" uses timbre. Say with your own voice the gliding, humming Why men, then pause a second, and explode the word crack. You hear the effect. It is the contrast between the smooth blend of W—m—n in why men and the sharp raucousness of the two k's combined with r in crack. The timbre of the voice weaves its effect among the other patterns of speech. Otherwise, the headline "Why men crack" concentrates within itself most of the power, the rhythm, and the feeling of the copy that follows. "Why men crack" has a short time duration, 0.98 seconds, that is almost identical with the time duration of "Strong men,"

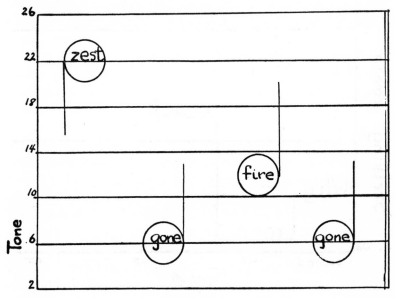

Figure 45

"vigorous men," "robust men." The headline commences the
even timing of phrases that sets the pattern for the steady pace
of the regular cadence of the march to destruction. It has the
same upswing in the pulse of striking power that rises and warns
as it barks: "they drive," "they drive," "they lash," "they crash."
The dynamic graph of "Why men crack" (Fig. 46) shows the
power of crack towers like a phonetic crag over the weaker words
in Why and men, and suggests, with this final volume of sound
the end point, the last step toward the terrible fall accumulating
during the process that will ultimately strike down the victims of
caffein.

Like the fall of stones, the breakdown of the nervous system
may be measured by the height of its plunge to destruction.

We have phonetically analyzed how a famous advertisement
presented the progression of the crackups brought on by over-

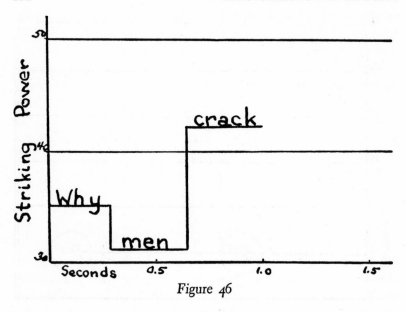

Figure 46

work and the stimulation of caffein. Let us now look at the way an actual crackup of a man occurs under the direction of Shakespeare's genius.

Early in his career, Shakespeare was confronted with somewhat the same technical problem that faces many modern writers. He, too, began his literary career by writing for the printed page. The sonnets and "Venus and Adonis" were written years before his great tragedies. At twenty-five Shakespeare was an accomplished writer of the written word. Then, as a playwright and an owner of the Globe Theatre, he wrote his words for actors to speak from the stage. The stage compelled Shakespeare to break with some of his written-word habits and put rhythms of speech into his language. His technical problem was not too different from the adjustment of the newspaper or magazine writer who suddenly must produce scripts for the radio or video; or the novelist who decides to write for the stage or the screen. One of the reasons for the immortality of Shakespeare's art is that great literature is preserved in printed words, and profound observations can be performed as a show.

Our speech differs from the Elizabethan's, yet the modern reader can hear the meters and rhythms in a Shakespearean play. Twentieth-century actors and their audiences perceive an unambiguous beauty in Shakespearean language. Evidently the permanence of the auditory quality in a writer's language depends on the length of time that his phonetic patterns can be heard in spite of the changes in his countrymen's speech.

The crackup passage we shall phonetically analyze is the melodramatic scene from *King Lear* when the old king insanely wanders about in an open field under claps of thunder and torrential rain. As the reader may recall, this scene occurs toward the middle of the play. Lear had stupidly given away his kingdom to the daughters who despised him, and had disinherited the one daughter who sincerely loved him. The hour for the payment of his blunder arrived with violence. It was a tempest on a wild night. The two daughters, who now owned the whole land, had refused him shelter from the elements. Like an unwanted cur, he found himself kicked out into the storm. A series of images in the following passage proclaim that Man's ingratitude to Man is inherent in Nature. The images subtly compare the madness of Lear with the cataclysmic violence of the storm, as he raves against "the rack of this tough world."

> Blow, winds, and crack your cheeks! Rage! Blow!
> You cataracts and hurricanoes, spout
> 'Till you have drenched our steeples, drowned the cocks!
> You sulphurous and thought-executing fires
> Vaunt-coureers to oak-cleaving thunderbolts,
> Singe my white head! And thou, all-shaking thunder,
> Smite flat the thick rotundity o' the world!
> Crack nature's moulds, all germins spill at once
> That make ingrateful man!

It is a comment upon our own mental limitations that Shakespeare's endowment of natural forces with the characteristics of human behavior is not the last appearance in history of the imitative magic of the primitive mind. The twentieth-century author of "Why Men Crack" also traffics with magic when he quotes from physics: "For every action there is an equal and opposite reaction," and then propounds that the human body's reactions to caffein stimulation are explained by Newton's law of motion. Both the modern advertisement writer and the Elizabethan dramatist are attempting verbally to color the eyes of people into believing that a metaphor is a natural law. There is just as much scientific justification for identifying the human body with the molecules and planets of physics as there is for Shakespeare to shock his audience with a staged thunderstorm into feeling the horrible fate of Lear obeys some vast cosmic principle. Both writers are presenting fictions as though they were scientific facts in order to convince an audience. Such fabrications are technical fantasies. They satisfy Man's desire to feel at home in the universe, and their appeal is founded upon that somewhat profound impulse that leads men to make myths, cosmic systems, and religions.

"Blow, winds, and crack your cheeks! Rage! Blow!" is bombast that depends on ringing words for its effect. Six out of eight of these words are charged with the highest levels of striking power: Blow . . . winds . . . crack . . . cheeks . . . rage . . . blow. The other two words: and . . . your are average. That assumes they would be slurred in this context with schwa ə vowels. If the words "and," "your" were spoken slowly, clearly and deliberately, they would make the rhetoric still louder. There is not one extremely weak word in the whole line. Five of the words are punctuated with commas and exclamation marks that stop the monologue's flow. These pauses permit the mind's ear to concentrate its attention on short bursts of speech in single words whose time durations have been whittled down to the limits for

maximum loudness. The spatial separations between the tone
plateaus of *blow* and *winds, your* and *cheeks, rage* and *blow* are
wide. The effect makes these words strike extra clear tones. The
graph of Figure 47 shows that the tone and power waves of this

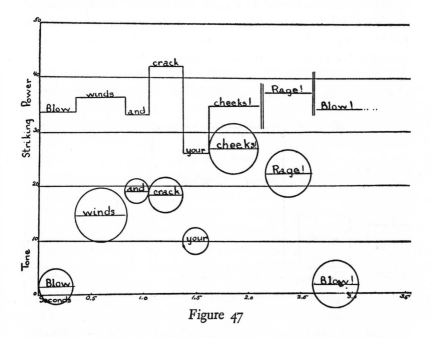

Figure 47

line move in the same direction and have a similar shape and,
therefore, give to each other a remarkable amount of support.
This may be one of the loudest sentences in English literature.

Notice how Shakespeare cuts the length of the above sentence
to eight syllables instead of the usual ten in blank verse. He is
tailoring (consciously or unconsciously) the speaking time to the
approximate time duration of the other lines in the script. This
is Shakespeare, the showman, considering the speech rate of his
actors performing on the stage. Yet Shakespeare, the writer,
stylizes most of this line with the regular blank verse cadence

of Elizabethan poetry: (weak syllable—strong syllable) plus (weak syllable—strong syllable) plus (weak syllable—strong syllable). Observe the end of the line of Figure 47. There the power level of *blow* falls relative to *rage*. That is how Shakespeare introduces rhythmic variety and breaks the monotony of mechanical blank verse. You can hear a balance of power in the phrasing of the line. Word power is evenly distributed. The symmetry of these time durations sustains this balance.

The ear detects a pacing in the time differences among the phrases in the sentence in Figure 48, a pacing that makes

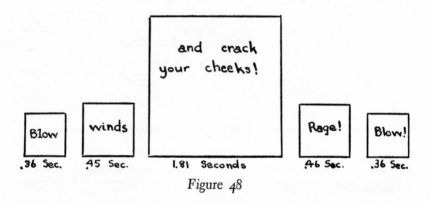

Figure 48

rhythm. Observe how feeling can be conveyed by variations in the flow of discourse:

    0.36   0.45   1.21 seconds   0.46   0.36
    "Blow, winds, (and crack your cheeks)! Rage! Blow!

These exclamatory breaks and changes in the pace of speech not only direct the reader-listener's attention toward the outbursts of phonetic power that Shakespeare put into his words and syllables. They are signs of excitement and symbols of the broken, fragmented emotions erupted in the explosion of Lear's mind. The phrase timing is Shakespeare, the dramatist, directing his actors to get across to the public the expressive power that Shakespeare, the poet, wrote into his words.

The diagram in Figure 48 illustrates what we mean by the tracing of a phrase or a sentence. It is an ordering of proportions among the durations of continuous speech. These proportions relate the lengths of periods between starts and stops of discourse. Their pacing is nothing but a variation of ratios among segments of time. Because rhythm in language is any order of phonetic elements that fluctuate with time, the pacings of speech are not, when strictly considered, genuine rhythms. It is a senseless statement to assert that time is a function of time. Yet that is almost the implication of considering the periodicities of speech as rhythms. The pause-punctuated periods of speech break it up into durations of undifferentiated talk. Their chief contribution is to clarify the audibility of the power, tone, and timbre patterns and the meaning of sentences and phrases by adjusting the lengths of the outbursts of speech to the attention spans of the audience. The pacings of speech do allow pauses for breathing and for emphasis. Short sentences may affect psychological states such as excitement or impatience; long-enduring, rolling sentences may induce a sense of continuity and the smooth and serene. Because they are adjustments to attention spans, they are factors in the readability and listenability of writing. But it is the phonetic rhythm that carries most of the auditory load to the mind's ear. It creates the auditory intelligence in the script. What the frame is to the picture, or the arrangement to the musical score, so is the time-pacing to the phonetic patterns in the writing. That is why masters of periodic style are not for that reason the best makers of language music or memorable prose. And that is why some masters of the sounds of language, such as James Joyce, Proust, Thomas Wolfe, and occasionally Shakespeare, disregard the attention spans of the audience—and are difficult to read. This is no brief for a barbarous contempt for readability. It is a defense for the descriptive

content of the auditory signals in writing and an attempt to de-
lete illusions about the importance of the facile periodic style.
The slick is not necessarily the rich, and vice versa.

Figure 49 is another example of how an abrupt, terse phrase
permits words of inherently high phonetic power to realize their

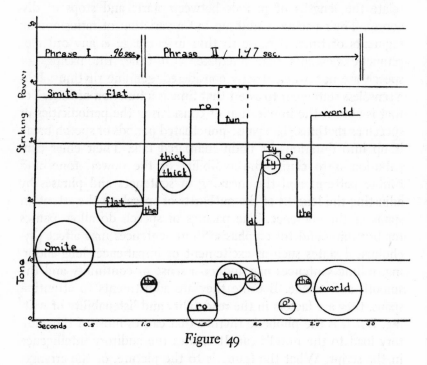

Figure 49

potential strength and strike the listener's ear with a maximum
impact.

The phrase "Smite flat" is juxtaposed to the phrase "the thick
rotundity o' the world." The latter has considerably more duration and less striking power. These contrasts in timing and loudness reinforce the contrast in meaning between flatness and
rotundity, and are compatible with the idea of the leveling of
the earth. The extra power of "Smite flat" places the emphasis
where it belongs. Other phonetic factors that create a pause after

flat are the stop consonant *t*, and the time consumed in suddenly lowering the tongue to articulate *the* immediately after the upswing of the voice in "Smite flat." These phonetic shifts synchronize with the rhythms of feeling signaled by the meaning of the words.

Actors who must choose between stressing the power or the contradictory tonal patterns of *rotundity* should keep one acoustic fact in mind. Our hearing of tones, vowel tones included, becomes clearer the longer they endure in time. The average 0.12-second and 0.07-second vowels in the last three syllables of *rotundity* are short. The transciency of all the short vowels, ə, ĭ, ŭ, ĕ reduces the hearing of their tones. This supports the other factors that make the power patterns of words capture the auditory channels to the brain. Therefore, the dynamic rhythm of *rotundity* will tend to dominate hearing. On the other hand, the three words, "o' the world," that end the line, run along on the same low tonal plane. All the consonants and semivowels that flank their low vowels have a low-tone influence. The duration of *world* is long. Therefore, if an actor cares to drop the pitch of his voice at the end of the line, his inflection will still more effectively express the feeling for the leveling of the earth that the dynamic pattern elsewhere projects.

The dynamic rhythms of syllables, because they are clearest to the ear, can produce the widest assortment of phonetic patterns that will affect an audience. They give the writer the greatest opportunity to create audio-scriptic intelligence. We expect, and we do find, that Shakespeare uses these richer forms of language. The graph (Fig. 50) of "drenched our steeples, drowned the cocks" reveals rhythmic patterns that suggest the form and outline of things and actions that Shakespeare wanted to express.

The form of meter, shock of pause, and words that shout with power through phrases balanced in time are not the whole story of Shakespeare's phonetic art. Nor did his intuitive skill to construct representational images with the power-time patterns of syllables exhaust the technical resources at his disposal. Shake-

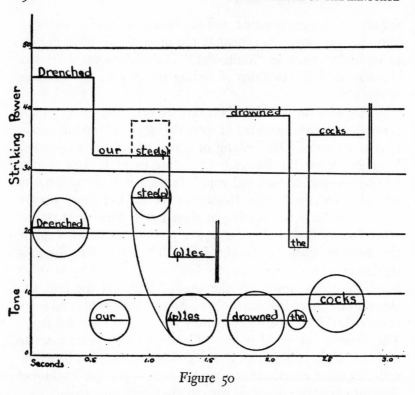

Figure 50

speare, the poet, was trained to hear the tone rhythms and timbres of speech. The printing press had not yet separated poetry
from music and speech was rhetorical. The Elizabethan stage
was full of song. The audience had auditory imagination. It was
"good theatre" to make words sing. A gifted craftsman like
Shakespeare could, and frequently did, enrich his manuscripts
with the timbre of consonants and the melodious tone rhythms
of the full-voiced vowels.

If a stage director were to hand an actor a diagram of both
the power and tone patterns of the passage presented in Figure
51, he would be giving the actor phonetic outlines that suggest
a variety of interpretations of:

131

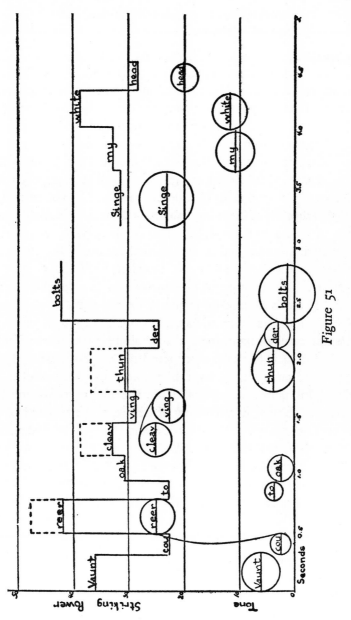

Figure 51

> Vaunt-coureers to oak-cleaving thunder bolts,
> Singe my white head!

One interpretation is to follow those tone patterns which the dynamic orientations favor, i.e., "coureer → oak-cleaving," coureer or "coo rǐ ā" being the earlier French pronunciation of courier. These sequences spring the high, intense, and keen tones of reer and cleaving up from the steady, low-tone level of the syllabic environment. If courier is pronounced coo rǐ ā the same effect is enhanced. Nor does the somewhat regular power of the words (other than reer) interfere. Furthermore, the vowel overtones in oo and ee or ǐā and "oh" produce a tonal beat. This sudden eruption of high and melodious tones is ideal for some types of voices to suggest the echo of the occasional music in reverberant thunder and to express that feeling of the sharp, the quick, and the keen which we associate with the cleaving of lightning. This interpretation emphasizes the tonality of the words. There is also an opportunity for the actor to stress with the timbre of k in coureer, oak, cleaving; and the t in vaunt, to, bolts, the crack of lightning and the splintering of trees. Another interpretation is to make every word in "singe my white head" hold to the same steady, level, high pitch that is inherent in the script. This performance would use the phrase as a symbol of hysteria as though it were a cry of desperation rising out of the low rumbling tones of the storm among the bolts of destruction. The graph shows this is possible solely because not one word in "singe my white head" is low-toned. Actually, the phrase has a dominant power rhythm. Therefore, it is necessary to hold the duration of each word longer than normal in order to develop clearly the hysterical tone. A more natural rendition is the dy-

39.5

namic one. The pattern shows white is acoustically more power-

32.0   28.5

ful than singe. . . . And head ends the phrase with a dying down in power that could express both phonetically and histrionically a sense of self-pity or weakness or despair. Here the helplessness of old age that contributed to Lear's tragedy would be voiced.

These examples show how graphs of this kind may stimulate the vocal and auditory imagination of the actor without curtailing his freedom as an artist. It is to be noticed that these patterns do not give commands to actors; they suggest possibilities.

The analyses presented show that the training of the poet and the experience of the dramatist sensitized the hearing of Shakespeare with diversified forms of phonetic intelligence. All varieties of the dynamics and the tone rhythms of language were at his command. It is not accidental that among the masters of classical Greek, French, and Spanish literature the most immortal artists began their literary careers as poets. A poet's training was a prerequisite for writing the dramas of ancient Greece. Plato was a dramatist early in life. The author of *Don Quixote* tried to write for the Spanish stage years before he created his world-famous romance of adventure, thought, and sorrow. Verse was the language of the Spanish theater of the sixteenth century. Cervantes, who died on the same day as Shakespeare, was a poet in his youth. Molière, the greatest comic dramatist of Europe, although he failed miserably as a young writer of tragedy for the classic French theater, learned much of his literary craft through his efforts to write poetic drama. And England produced the master of linguistic eloquence in Shakespeare, first as a poet, second as a dramatist, and later in life a consummation of both.

We can learn a lesson from the great masters of literature. The masterpieces that have stood the test of time and endured through the vagaries of fashion down through the last 2,500 years possess certain common technical characteristics. Their language combined the visual image of the printed word and the sound image of conversational speech. The great masters frequently were writers of poetic drama that developed and matured their visual and auditory intelligence. Now, after more than two centuries of the printed muted word, devoid of sound imagery and therefore deleted of feeling, will radio and televised speech restore, at least technically, some of the lost intelligence of great literature?

10

Possibilities

ON THE SURFACE, IT SEEMS OBVIOUS THAT THE MORE A BRANCH OF writing is involved with sound, the more direct will be the application of these techniques. This apparent fact must be qualified by considering the nature and the power of the sounds with which the writing is associated. The song writer will be helped by information about the relative durations of the syllables he must synchronize with the time pattern of his musical notes. A grasp of the factors that produce the power patterns of natural speech will assist the lyricist to make the rhythms of his words correspond more closely with the dynamic and melodic rhythms of his music. But the quality of the tones discussed in this book are not the tone quality of the singing voice or of musical instruments.

The radio and video script writer, the poet and librettist, will acquire more technical skill and more mastery over their art through knowledge of how to construct audio-visual patterns with the sounds carried by words. This, too, is obvious.

But audio-scriptic intelligence isolates and abstracts those elements of speech that the writer is able to use, and only those. It does not include shouted or highly intonated speech. Furthermore, the nature of the sounds at the disposal of the writer are weak in comparison with declamatory speech, the singing voice, and the tonal organizations of orchestral instruments. This was demonstrated, quantitatively, by Figure 3. Accordingly, *phonetic intelligence will contribute most to those writers who produce both for silent and oral reading.* Its most effective signals are for reader-listeners. Therefore, these techniques will be extremely serviceable to the playwright who needs more mastery over idioms of speech, analytically and constructively, and who wishes his play to be read as literature. The same service extends to all writers of dialogue whether they work in the field of the short story, the novel, video, radio, or motion pictures. Sound images based on the syllabic and word rhythms of power, tone, and timbre that draw feelings from the origins of oral memory are vital material for writers of poetic prose in advertising copy, fiction, and the drama. These instruments will help these writers. The literary stylist who relies on rhythm for his art will be aided by these techniques. Another possible field for these methods is the translation of foreign poetry and highly stylized prose. Because patterns of tone and striking power carry the feelings rather than specific vowels and consonants, these forms might give the translator a phonetic model to guide the rhythms of his writing.

There can be a strictly experimental field of phonetic writing, providing the interests of writers are set up as the standards for evaluation. These interests are:

What themes or subject matter and what areas of experience can the different types of phonetic signals most aptly express? This is the quest of the writer "fishing for the right word" expanded into a search for the most appropriate phonetic pattern. Since what a writer has to say is the principal measure of his accomplishment, an appraisal of subject matter in the light of its most appropriate signals should bring the mind of the writer closer to his basic interests: what he has to say. History of the descriptive arts shows there is interdependence between descriptive power and scope of subject matter.

A second departure point for experimentation is the question: "In what branches or types of writing will the signals of phonetic intelligence give the most service to the writer? This requires evaluations of the numerous fields of writing by experienced producers with some technical imagination.

Another line of investigation is to evaluate the impacts of the signals of phonetic patterns on groups of people differing in age, auditory background, verbal training, and social mood. The prevailing social mood is the most important factor because it influences all changes in the styles of writing, phonetic styles included. This approach may interest publishers more than writers.

Once these standards of interest are established, there is some point to investigating the acoustic nature and the sound dimensions of signals carried by auditory patterns to reader-listeners.

The importance of structure in phonetic signals has been stressed. Those interested in experimenting with these phonetic techniques will naturally wish to know their pattern potential, or the number of their possible combinations.

The maximum number of possible dynamic patterns for a ten-syllable sentence with three levels of discernible striking power is 2,187. This calculation allocates one pattern to every three syllables. If the reader-listener can discriminate four levels of striking power in a similar ten-syllable system there are 19,683 possible striking-power patterns. Between three and four degrees of striking power among syllables will give approximately 10,000 different patterns. The deviations of the average reader-listener's judgment of loudness make this figure a rough estimate of the outside case of pattern possibility on a dynamic basis. Within the limits of a ten-syllable sentence the number of possible tone structures will be fewer. A writer can establish three clear levels of tone in a ten-syllable sentence if the dynamic level is kept constant. This quite special case, that usually needs some rhyme for unmistakable clarity, would yield a maximum of 2,187 tone patterns. When the tone and dynamic patterns follow the same direction and have the same shape, no extra formal patterns are added to those established by the dynamics.

It is understood that these numbers for pattern potentials are outside cases. They do not consider the restrictions in choice imposed on the writer by the meanings of words and the orders of grammar and syntax. They are completely valid for nonsense writing such as boogiewoogie lyrics. The number of these pattern combinations explains how it could come about that a writer such as James Joyce wrote fluently and copiously on a strictly phonetic emotional plane without concern for conventional meaning. Naturally, writers who invent a private language of feeling with sound images will be understood only by those who have the time and inclination to learn their personal language.

The duration of a single act of attention by a reader may range from three to twenty-four seconds. The usual duration lasts between five and eight seconds. These periods of perception mean the writer can count on twenty-five to thirty successive syllables as the limit for establishing the effects of phonetic patterns. Within this limit the possible number of pattern combinations are so numerous that meaning need not be sacrificed to develop audio-scriptic intelligence. The number is so enormous that the mind alone cannot use these curves as though they were parts of a mechanical system. For practical purposes the number of patterns approaches infinity.

Can a system for rating the phonetic intelligence of advertising copy be established? Only under these conditions: agreement in advance on what emotions or feelings are to be induced in the minds of selected groups of potential buyers; the compatibility of the commodity and its brand name with the tone of these emotions; the price and laborsaving appeals of the commodity or service to be sold; the prevailing social emotions of the test groups. Let us call these conditions the over-all appeals of the advertisement. If the over-all appeals of an advertisement are clearly defined and stabilized, then the contributions of auditory intelligence to the effectiveness of the copy may be isolated and estimated. "Stabilized" means the number of times an ad appears through one channel of communication, such as a radio station, magazine, or newspaper. It is taken for granted that the quality of performance will be approximately the same throughout the experiment. Sales results of specific ads using different phonetic forms can then be evaluated. At least six months of careful experimentation and correlation should show results that are significant. But no such experimentation can even be begun without an explicit agreement in advance on the over-all appeals of the copy. Phonetic patterns are tools to make verbal communication more effective. They are not cookbook recipes, literary machines, or patented formulas. It is predicted that the emotional aura carried by a brand name will be a phonetic factor of some weight. If Mr. Schmalz Grimes wants to go into the perfume business, that is his capital privilege. However, the delicacy and the sexual aroma of a perfume will not be signaled by calling it "Schmalz Grimes."

The use of these phonetic patterns to make copy "effective" brings the technique of writing as close as possible to the fields of performance. The goal of the writing is reduced to a single activity: to sell. The audience is visualized as a group of buyers, consciously appraised and clearly defined. When the conception of a probable audience or reader-listener becomes less definite, fewer adjustments are required of the writer. The reader-listener must make more of the adjustments. "Originality" in the fields of fiction, drama, and poetry occurs when the writer creates his own audience, as a leader, not as a follower. Although the sales interests of publishers restrict this freedom of the writer more rigidly than ever before, this opportunity remains the dream of many writers.

Whether a writer wishes to voice a protest against excessive mechanization or the imperfections of Nature, or eulogize personal freedom, or express the fatefulness of social forces, feature the call of the wild in the He-Man, these phonetic techniques can refine and clarify the feelings and tone of his language. Under certain circumstances, as in the auditory imagination of the poet, they may evoke profound emotional images that spring up with the freshness of a startling discovery and revitalize memories otherwise lost.

The subjective use of these techniques may be their most valuable contribution to the writer.

These methods will enlarge the hearing of some writers, but should not be used as substitutes for hearing by any writer. They do not give to the auditory imagination of an author the subtly dissonant or euphonious effects caused by all neighboring vowel overtones. They do not show the masking and resonating effects of adjacent consonants, vowels, and semivowels. They do not fully reveal the slow growth and the "dying fall" within the period of articulating a single vowel sound, i.e., peak powers. These techniques do give the writer these things: a finer understanding and greater control over the broad contours of energy in syllables and words. They show reasons why we tend to hear phonetic patterns as a tonal impression or as a fluctuation of vocal noise. They present some of the more minute qualities of speech we hear within syllables and words. These qualities, or casts of the voice, have been classified, organized, and simplified as an orchestra of the language that places them more directly at the disposal of the writer.

The hearing of some animals covers a wider range of frequency than the hearing of man. Instruments detect and record intensities and frequencies that the human ear cannot resolve. But within the range of our hearing few animals are as sensitive and none can organize what they do hear with the intelligence of men. The magnified portrayals of sound recorded on precision instruments are answers to questions that men asked. The mind is the Sesame to our hearing of patterns moving clearly through music and vaguely through speech, patterns that become more definite with audio-visual techniques.

Here two connected questions arise: How much time and work are required to master these procedures? Are these techniques really helpful to a writer with a fine ear? Shakespeare managed to do quite well without tables, diagrams, graphs, etc.

Let us confront the time question first. Some writers specialize in short compositions. These are the writers of advertising copy, blurbs, titles, songs, television or radio announcements, and poetry. These writers can afford to spend the time to concentrate on auditory perfection; and they can use these techniques completely. But novelists, dramatists, and authors of nonfiction books will have the time to use these techniques only on short or especially important passages. For these writers, audio-scriptic intelligence has two main services to offer: as a thesaurus, and as a conditioner of auditory or phonetic habits. After a single page of data has been understood and used (Table 1, Part II) it becomes a part of auditory memory. Then diagrams and charts need not be drawn. They become references, supplemented by examples in the book. The same development will occur for all writers who read the book and do a reasonable amount of experimentation with its analytical and compositional techniques. If a writer has a good ear, the time required to use these procedures will be far less than for writers handicapped by inferior auditory sensitivity. But the latter are the ones who have the most need for these methods, which brings us back to Shakespeare. The fact that an exceptional genius is gifted with amazing auditory intelligence should not deny to the majority of writers an opportunity to refine their phonetic skills. A mass society, in contrast to a class society, must raise the general level in order to flourish. Therefore, any techniques that may augment the hearing of language among a sizable number of writers (and ultimately readers) has some service to give.

Nor should the new channels for experimentation opened up by these techniques be slighted. For this purpose the experimental work of writers will be of critical importance.

The quantitative aspects of these processes will liberate the technical imagination of writers who have scientific inclinations. These writers undoubtedly will realize that the quantities used are standardizations and all standardizations sacrifice some details. That is the price paid for science, whether it be applied to matter or to society or, in this case, to auditory elements in writing. It is a human predicament to be uncertain about changes in detail throughout a process while pattern is focused upon. And, vice versa, while details are the point of attention, the over-all structure is frequently lost sight of. If these reservations are kept in mind, then the phonetic patterns analyzed or developed by a writer will be listened to as guides to hearing, not as auditory crutches or mechanical hearing aids. There is, for us, no finer, no more sensitive recorder of sounds than the human ear itself. We have no richer recording of the voice than speech heard. These techniques are refinements of the natural and the spontaneous—not substitutes for them.

Part II

Tables for Giving Phonetic Values
to Words

Diacritical Markings	Diacritical Markings

Vowels

ă *in* cat
ah *in* father, embalm
ā *in* fame, rain, pay, seine
aw *in* all, saw, pause
ĕ *in* ebb
ee *in* see, tea, field, pique, Pete
er *in* her, fur, world, stir
ĭ *in* is
ī *in* pine, sigh, my, eye, lie
oh *in* old, moan, sew, tow, own
ow *in* howl, bough
oo *in* ooze, tune, tomb, two, blue,
    flew
oi *in* oil
ŏŏ *in* book, could, put
ew *in* few, you, muse
ŭ *in* sun, won
ə *in* the

Consonants

b
d
f
g
h
j *in* judge, George
k
l
m
n
p
r
s
t
dh *in* then
th *in* thin
ch *in* church, witch
sh *in* show
ng *in* sing
zh *in* pleasure, azure
v
w
y *in* you
z

TABLE 1 *

Summary of Phonetic Values with Diacritical Markings

Phonetic Element	Relative Striking Power Value	Relative Mean Time in Seconds	Subscript 1 is prevowel, subscript 2 postvowel
ī in pine, sigh, my	30	0.22 Sec.	
oi in oil, toy	30	.22	
aw in all, saw, pause	29	.17	
ah in father, embalm	28	.17	
ă in cat	28	.17	
oh in old, moan, sew	28	.17	
ā in fame, rain, pay	28	.22	
ew in few, you, muse	28	.17	
ŭ in sun, won	27	.12	
ee in see, tea, field	26	.17	
ĕ in ebb	25	.12	
ow in howl, bough	24	.22	
ĭ in is	24	.12	
er in her, fur, world	23	.17	
oo in ooze, tune, blue	20	.17	
ŏŏ in book, could, put	19	.12	
ə in the	15	.07	
r	8	.07	
l	5	.07	
w	5	.07	
ch in church, witch	5	ch_1 .07	ch_2 0.17
ng in sing	4	.14	
sh in show	4	.12	
y in you	4	.07	
n	3	n_1 .07	n_2 .12

* This table sums up numerically all the phonetic values in this book. Because of its economy and comprehensiveness it will be the table most frequently used. Part I of this book can be considered the theory, the explanation, and the preparation to use the data of this table.

TABLE 1—*Continued*

Phonetic Element		Relative Striking Power Value	Relative Mean Time in Seconds		Subscript 1 is prevowel, subscript 2 postvowel	
m		3	m_1	.12	m_2	.14
j	*in* judge, George	3		.17		
zh	*in* pleasure, azure	3	zh_1	.07	zh_2	.12
dh	*in* then	3	dh_1	.07	dh_2	.12
z		3	z_1	.12	z_2	.14
g		3		.12		
k		3	k_1	.02	k_2	.07
t		3	t_1	.02	t_2	.07
f		2		.12		
v		2	v_1	.07	v_2	.12
d		2		.07		
b		2		.12		
p		2	p_1	.02	p_2	.07
s		2		.12		
h		1.5		.07		
th	*in* thin	1		.12		

Relative Tone Level of Vowels		Effects of Neighboring Consonants on Vowels	No Effect: h, k, g, ng
oo, oh	2	Low: f, v, p, b, m, l	
ŏŏ, er	4		
aw, ow, ə, ŭ	6		
ah	8	Middle Low: r, w, th, dh	
ew, oi	10		
ī	12		
ă	19	Middle High: h, d, n, z, t	
ĕ	21		
ā	22		
ĭ	24	High: s, ch, sh, zh, y, j	
ee	26		

TABLE 2 *

Summary of Phonetic Values For International Phonetic Alphabet

Phonetic Element	Relative Striking Power Value	Relative Mean Time in Seconds	Subscript 1 is prevowel Subscript 2 postvowel
aɪ *in* pine	30	0.22	
ɔɪ *in* oil	30	.22	
ɔ *in* all	29	.17	
a *in* father	28	.17	
æ *in* cat	28	.17	
o *in* old	28	.17	
eɪ *in* fame	28	.22	
ɪu *in* you	28	.17	
ʌ *in* sun	27	.12	
i *in* see	26	.17	
e *in* ebb	25	.12	
av *in* howl	24	.22	
ɪ *in* is	24	.12	
ɵ *in* her	23	.17	
u *in* ooze	20	.17	
v *in* book	19	.12	
ə *in* the	15	.07	
r	8	.07	
l	5	.07	
w	5	.07	
tʃ *in* church	5	tʃ₁ .07	tʃ₂ 0.17
ŋ *in* sing	4	.14	
ʃ *in* show	4	.12	
j *in* you	4	.07	
n	3	n₁ .07	n₂ .12

* This table expresses the same data as Table 1, with the International Phonetic Alphabet.

TABLE 2—Continued

Phonetic Element		Relative Striking Power Value	Relative Mean Time in Seconds		Subscript 1 is prevowel, subscript 2 postvowel	
m		3	m_1	.12	n_2	.14
dʒ	in judge	3		.17		
ʒ	in pleasure	3	$dʒ_1$	.07	$dʒ_2$	.12
ð	in then	3	$ə_1$	.07	$ə_2$	.12
z		3	z_1	.12	z_2	.14
g		3		.12		
k		3	k_1	.02	k_2	.07
t		3	t_1	.02	t_2	.07
f		2		.12		
v		2	v_1	.07	v_2	.12
d		2		.07		
b		2		.12		
p		2	p_1	.02	p_2	.07
s		2		.12		
h		1.5		.07		
θ	in thin	1		.12		

Relative Tone Level of Vowels		Effects of Neighboring Consonants on Vowels	No effect: h, k, g, ng
v, ɔ	2	Low, f, v, p, b, m, l	
u, o	4		
ɔ, av, ə, ʌ	6		
o	8	Middle Low, ɪ, w, θ, ð	
ɪu, ɔɪ	10		
aɪ	12		
æ	19	Middle High, d, n, z, t	
e	21		
eɪ	22		
ɪ	24	High, s, tʃ, ʃ, j, dʒ, ʒ	
i	26		

Notes For Using Table 3

When a consonant is marked with the suffix 1, it indicates that the consonant precedes a vowel: as p_1, k_1, t_1.

When a consonant is marked with the suffix 2, it indicates that the consonant follows a vowel: as p_2, k_2, t_2.

Rules for Constructing Short and Long Words with Table 3

In using the rules for constructing short and long words you must remember these six numbers: 0.02 seconds

0.07

0.12

0.14

0.17

0.22

These numbers are the average durations of groups of speech sounds. The average duration of a word is the sum of its component numbers. The numbers are classifications. The reason for the classifications is simplicity. The speech sounds within the groups represented by these six numbers have twenty different average time durations. It is too cumbersome for a writer to use twenty numbers to calculate the average time of a syllable or word. The time patterns of phrases and sentences will be negligibly affected by this practical simplification. If a writer wants a device to fix these numbers in his memory, eliminate 0.14. The remaining numbers: 0.02—0.07—0.12—0.17—0.22 are separated by 0.05-second intervals.

0.02 represents the shortest speech sounds, k_1, p_1, t_1 in Group 1.

0.22 represents the duration of the longest sounds, the diphthongs, ā, ow, oi, ī in Group 6.

Rules for making short words:

1. Combine the short consonants in Groups 1 and 2 with the swift vowels in Groups 2 and 3.
2. Use the fewest possible number of consonants.

Rules for making long words:

1. Combine the long-enduring consonants in Groups 3, 4, 5 with the long diphthongs in Group 6.
2. Use the greatest possible number of consonants with either vowels in Group 5 or the diphthongs in Group 6.

TABLE 3

AVERAGE TIME DURATION OF GROUPS OF VOWELS AND CONSONANTS
OF GENERAL AMERICAN SPEECH AT A SPEAKING RATE
OF 148 WORDS PER MINUTE

Shortest Time Duration				*Longest Time Duration*	
Group 1 Average 0.02 Sec.	Group 2 Average 0.07 Sec.	Group 3 Average 0.12 Sec.	Group 4 Average 0.14 Sec.	Group 5 Average 0.17 Sec.	Group 6 Average 0.22 Sec.
p_1 0.02	k_2 0.05	m_1 0.10	m_2 0.14	ew 0.16	$\bar{a}$ 0.21
k_1 .03	ə .06	n_2 .10	z_2 .15	ee .16	ow .22
t_1 .03	t_2 .06	g .10	ng .15	j .17	oi .22
	n_1 .06	z_1 .11		er .17	$\bar{\imath}$ .23
	l .07	th .11		aw .17	
	w .07	ŏŏ .11		ch_2 .17	
	r .07	b .11		ă .17	
	d .08	f .12		oo .18	
	p_2 .08	sh .12		ah .19	
	dth_1 .08	ĭ .12		oh .19	
	v_1 .08	ĕ .12			
	zh_1 .08	v_2 .12			
	ch_1 .09	zh_2 .12			
	y .09	dth_2 .12			
	h .09	s .13			
		ŭ .13			

NOTE: The writer's judgment must decide whether a sound is to be shared between two adjacent words or syllables. Judgments of this kind depend on understanding when the voice will probably slur certain sequences of sounds. When speech does slur, an allocation of half of the sound's duration to each of the two syllables or words involved will not destroy the time pattern. Slurring also depends on the interest and emphasis that a probable reader-listener will give to specific words. That is why only the writer's judgment can decide this doubtful case. Similar auditory skill is needed to select the shorter or longer time number of a consonant that occurs in a cluster. Examples of clusters are: (nts) in gents, (chd) in matched, (rmz) in farms, (spr) in spring. The voice has a tendency to slur sounds that occur in such clusters. Accordingly, it is more accurate to use the shorter duration values in these cases.

SUGGESTIONS FOR USING TIME NUMBERS

A. The time numbers to remember are: 0.20 seconds, 0.30 seconds, and 0.40 seconds.

  Monosyllabic words or single syllables with less than 0.20 seconds durations are the extremely swift ones.

  Durations between 0.20 and 0.30 seconds are also short in time.

  Extensions between 0.30 and 0.40 seconds are medium durations.

  Words and syllables over 0.40 seconds are long ones.

  There are syllables whose spoken time may extend over 0.50 seconds. These are unusual.

B. A syllable that falls on a pause at the end of a phrase or sentence extends longer in time, providing the vowel is not terminated by a stop consonant such as t, k, p. This extra duration will vary between 5 per cent and 80 per cent, depending on the nature of the vowel and the emphasis of thought and feeling. A third is not a misleading calculation for this increment, and the writer should always consider adding one third of its value to the time number of a terminal syllable whose voiced vibration is undamped by a stop consonant. If the writer's ear tells him that one third is too little or too much he should follow his own judgment. Whatever his estimation, he should not increase the time number more than 80 per cent.

C. Although a word of long duration usually has a large striking power, this does not always occur. There are short, loud words and prolonged medium-powered ones. Training is required to distinguish between the striking power and time duration of speech.

D. To calculate the speaking time of a phrase or sentence add the time numbers on all the syllables of the sentence or phrase.

E. The speaking rate determines the specific duration of words. *REMEMBER, THE PHONETIC INTELLIGENCE OF THE WRITER DEPENDS ON THE RELATIVE DURATIONS OF*

*SPEECH SOUNDS, NOT THEIR TOTAL TIME UNDER
SPECIAL CONDITIONS, SUCH AS AN AFTERDINNER
SPEECH.* The relationship of the time of one word to another
is unchanged regardless of the speaking rate. If you speak twice
as fast (296 words per minute) as the speaking rate used in this
dictionary (148 words per minute), the average duration of each
word is one half as long. If you talk with half the speed (74 words
per minute), the time consumed by each word will be doubled.
In either case the ratio of the duration of one word to another
remains the same. The time pattern is unaltered. Whatever negligible differences may exist, they are of no practical value to the
writer.

SUGGESTIONS FOR USING STRIKING-POWER NUMBERS

A. Keep these numbers in mind: 10—20—30—40. When you see a
striking-power number between 10 and 20, the syllable is extremely
weak. Numbers between 20 and 30 indicate average syllabic power.
Striking-power numbers over 30, especially in the neighborhood
of 40, represent the louder syllables. Numbers over 40 signify
syllables that have exceptionally high striking power.

B. Do not overtax the striking-power numbers or expect too much
discrimination of loudness in words by readers. The average person's ability to clearly hear a difference in striking power between
two syllables depends on a difference of seven striking-power
numbers. Highly sensitive ears, trained ears, may distinguish a
difference between two syllables separated by three numbers. This
is fine hearing. Count on the average person, the reader who will
not discriminate power differences among syllables unless they are
separated by seven units.

C. The maximum power differences between syllables rarely exceeds
twenty-eight units of striking power. Since a differential of seven
is necessary for discrimination this method reveals somewhere
between three and four levels of loudness or syllabic prominence.
Calculations are given for half a unit in order to show tendencies.

D. Where alternate pronunciations of words commonly occur, the
syllables will have different sounds. Therefore, some syllables in
some words have alternate striking-power numbers. Since these

variations in pronunciation depend on the position of the word in the sentence and on the way it is used, only the writer's judgment can decide which articulation is correct.

E. Do not concern yourself with the added striking power given to words by intonation and interpretation. You are not telling the actor or the speaker how to place accents or emphasize words. That is the actor's or director's or showman's responsibility. Write into your words the power, clarity, and definitiveness that only the writer can control. That is your job. You are creating the script for the show, not the show. Phonetic intelligence is designed to refine language. Its contributions to performance or showmanship lie outside the writer's control.

F. When you estimate the conventional (not interpretive) accents on two-syllable words, listen attentively. The voice distributes equal striking power to both syllables of some bisyllabic words, i.e.,

$$35\ 35 \qquad 36\ 36$$

farewell, carefree. And there are some two-syllable words that receive no extra accent of convention because the voice is not compelled to do extra work or to focus auditory attention on one of the two syllables: i.e., alone, alike, forty. These happen to be words whose two syllables show great differences in striking power. The context also has influence. In short, the writer must use extra auditory discrimination in allocating accents of convention to bisyllabic words. Remember these things about the accents of convention. They tend to fall on the syllable with the largest striking power number. That is the syllable with the greatest amount of natural phonetic power. This is a tendency . . . not a rule. When speech is very loud, the intrinsic striking powers of syllables tend to dominate hearing and mask the accent of convention. The writer of words that demand chanting, or shouting, or loud singing might remember this fact.

SUGGESTIONS FOR USING TABLE 4, STRIKING POWER

Rule 1. *Guides for Making Strong, Powerful Words.*

1.1 Use strong vowels for strong words or syllables, such as ī, oi, aw, ah, ā that have high numbers 30, 30, 29, 28, 28. These strong vowels border the area marked "most powerful" on

Table 4. The word *tight* is more powerful than the word *tout* because the vowel ī has more striking power than the vowel *ow*. Likewise, the word *boy* sounds louder than *burr* because the vowel *oi* is the stronger vowel.

1.2 Use the powerful semivowels r, l, w, y and the sounds ch, ng, and sh on the left side of the "most powerful" section of Table 4. The word *rile* is more conspicuously powerful than the word *dice* because its consonantal environment is stronger. *Law* is a more powerful word than *thaw* for the same reason.

1.3 Use as many consonants as possible to make accented, powerful words and syllables. For instance, the word *blithe* is louder and stronger than *buy* or *lie* because it possesses the vocal power of three consonants instead of one.

Rule 2. *Guides for Making Weak, Unaccented Syllables and Words.*

2.1 Use the quickly grunted, weak ə called the schwa. It appears in the extreme upper right-hand corner of the table's "minimum power" section. Use other weak, short vowels such as o͝o, oo, er, ĭ, ow, ĕ that appear above the same "minimum power" section. The values or numbers of the weak vowels lie between 15 and 25.

2.2 Use the weak consonants with striking power values between 1 and 3, such as th, s, p, d, k, etc. These appear on the left margin of the "minimum power" section.

2.3 Use words or syllables with the fewest possible number of consonants.

General Procedure: Combine the vowels and consonants in the "most powerful" section of the table to produce powerful words.

Combine the vowels and consonants in the least or "minimum power" area of the table to make weak words.

Remember the power of a syllable or a monosyllabic word is the sum of the powers of its phonetic elements. Naturally, the writer must hear accurately the sounds of speech, and must judge the phonetic values of words under the conditions of their use, i.e., their context.

STRIKING POWER

Consonants	Vowels →	30 (ai) I	30 (oi) oi	29 (ɔ) aw	28 (oe) ă	28 (a) ah	28 (o) oh	28 (ei) ā	28 (iu) ew	27 (ʌ) ŭ	26 (i) ee	25 (e) ĕ	24 (ev) ow	24 (l) ĭ	23 (ɚ) er	20 (u) oo	19 (v) ōō	15 (d) ɇ
8 (R) R		38	38	32	36	36	36	36	36	35	34							23
5 (L) L		35	35					33	33	32	31						/	/
5 (w) W		35						33	33	32	31						/	/
5 (tʃ) CH		35						33	33	32	31						/	/
4 (ŋ) NG		34						32	32	31	30						/	/
4 (ʃ) SH		34						32	32	31	30						/	/
4 (j) Y		34	34	33	32	32	32	32	32	31	30						/	/
3 (M) M																	22	/
3 (N) N																	22	/
3 (dʒ) J																	22	/
3 (ʒ) zh																	22	/
3 (ʃ) dth																	22	/
3 (z) z																	22	/
3 (G) G																	22	/
3 (K) K																	22	/
3 (T) T																	22	.
2 (F) F																	21	17
2 (V) V																	21	17
2 (B) B																	21	17
2 (D) D																	21	17
2 (P) P																	21	17
2 (s) S																	22	17
1½ (H) H																	20	16½
1 (θ) th		31	31	30	29	29	29	29	28	27	26	25	25	24	25		20	16

Most Powerful · Middle Power Area · Area of Minimum Power

Table 4

RULES FOR CONSTRUCTING THE TONES OF WORDS WITH TABLE 5

Rule 1. To make the words of highest tone combine the vowels and consonants in the section marked "highest tone" on the table. Examples are: *she, each, sage, say, sash, edge, sissie.*

Rule 2. To make the words of lowest tone combine the vowels and consonants in the section marked "lowest tone" on the table. Examples are: *fowl, fool, low, loaf, ball, pull, wool, move.*

Rule 3. To make the words of medium tone combine the vowels and consonants in the sections marked "middle high" and "middle low" on the table. Examples are: *dot, noise, writhe, die, knot, toy, done, wan, rot.*

Rule 4. When the high vowels are surrounded by two low-toned consonants or semivowels, subtract 1 from the tone number of the syllable or word. For example: the tone value of the vowel *ee* in *peel* is 26. Both consonants in the word have low-tone levels. Therefore 1 is subtracted from 26. The tone value of *peel* is 25.

Rule 5. When the high vowels occur in a syllable or word that contains only one consonant, and it is a low-toned consonant or semivowel, subtract ½ from the tone number of the word. For example: the tone value of the vowel *ĕ* in *ebb* is 21. The only consonant in the word is on a low tone level. Therefore ½ is subtracted from 21. The tone value of *ebb* is 20.5.

Rule 6. When the low vowels are surrounded by two high-toned consonants or semivowels, add 1 to the tone value of the syllable or word. For example: the tone value of the vowel *er* in *church* is 4. Both consonants in the word have high tone levels. Therefore 1 is added to 4. The tone value of *church* is 5.

Rule 7. When the low vowels occur in a syllable or word that contains only one consonant, and it is a high-toned consonant or semivowel, add ½ to the tone number of the word. For example: the tone value of the vowel *oh* in *Joe* is 2. The only consonant in the word is on a high tone level. Therefore ½ is added to 2. The tone value of *Joe* is 2.5.

Rule 8. When two consonants of opposite tone value surround a vowel in a syllable or word their tone influences neutralize each other. The tone value of the word is the tone value of the vowel. For example: the tone value of the vowel *ah* in *botch* is 8. The effect of the low-toned consonant *b* is neutralized by the effect of the high-toned consonant *ch*. The tone value of *botch* remains 8, which is the tone level of *ah*.

Rule 9. Disregard the tone influence of consonants and semivowels grouped under the sections marked "middle high" and "middle low" on the table. For practical purposes their influence is negligible. However, the user should be aware that spectroscopically there are differences.

NOTE 1. Remember most of the tone of words resides in the vowels.

NOTE 2. H, ng, k, g are not included in the tone table, because they exert no tone influence on vowels.

NOTE 3. Naturally, when both the consonants and the vowel in a word or syllable occupy the same tone level, that is the tone level of the word.

SUGGESTIONS FOR USING TONE NUMBERS

A. Remember these two numbers: 7—18.
   7 or less is a low-toned syllable.
   Between 7 and 13 is a middle-toned syllable or word.
   Above 18 is high to high-toned.

B. Repeat the same tone level at least three times in a sentence, if you want to make the tones in your language ring in the listener's ears. Bear in mind that most people do not listen to the tones of words. Even if they want to detect tonality, their ears are not trained to hear it. Therefore, a minimum of three out of ten successive syllables must possess the same tone to be effective. A less obvious technique for conveying the tones of words to your reader is to use tone numbers with the greatest possible difference in height. Another method, previously discussed, is to make the power pattern of your words follow suit with their tone pattern.

C. Writers of songs and jingles should disregard an alternate ə pronunciation when words are being written for the singing voice to vibrate clear vowel tones. Poets writing principally for the printed page will choose an alternate clear vowel or the ə pronunciation, according to their interests in the music of language or in the tone of natural conversation. The poet's phonetic intention will decide.

TONE VOCABULARY

	High Vowels					Middle Vowels				Low Vowels							
Consonant	26 ee	24 ǐ	22 ā	21 ě	19 ǎ	12 I	10 oi	10 iu	8 ah	6 ɔ	6 u	6 ow	6 aw	4 er	4 oo	2 oh	2 oo
High																	
sh																	
s		*Highest*															
ch		*Tone Words*															
zh in azure																	
Y																	
J																	
Middle High																	
D					*Middle High*												
N					*Tone Words*												
Z																	
T																	
Middle Low																	
R																	
W					*Middle Low*												
th					*Tone Words*												
dh in then																	
Low																	
F																	
V												*Lowest*					
P												*Tone Words*					
B																	
M																	
L																	

Table 5

Part III

Lyrics Composed with Techniques
Presented in this Book

ON WINDS AND WATERS

THE VOICE OF THE LONG RIVERS

The dominant background sound is one of uninterrupted running water. This is broken, sometimes drowned, by the overtones of human voices.

The tone quality of human speech, occasionally individual, other times choral, synchronizes, demonstrates, and features the onomatopoetic river sounds and images that make up the composition.

THE VOICE OF THE LONG RIVERS IN THE DELTA AND THE SOURCE

There was a humming in the mouth of lulls, mums, resonance,
Runs full of liquid mumblings, thrums,
Nodal nothings, undulants and blends.

There was a humming in the mouth of lulls, mums, thrums
Where the delta's resonance with shells
Descends

         down coral fledging walls . . . and, pursing
Ends
   the rivers' purlings in the turns
they left behind in lees.

Those swirls of turns in earth,

Their low reverberance of shelvings in the bends
Expand,
Whir on trembling films,
Endome and blur . . .

As though all memories of water, celled in a cup,
were merged with thin, celestial weather breath
on blue skeets past shoals,
where thermal lifted surfaces give up their undercurrent's pulse

Through vaporous holes above the seas . . .

To coolings in the ozone's ease.

But far . . .
Upstream

Roughness,
cropping from the gorged round-head source,

Rose the roar of water's raucousness,
where pourings quarry bars from breaking quartz off rocks
in rolling boulders towards the seas;

Where roarings of the pour
(rolling boulders towards the seas)
Soften
with that covering, bubbling, frothing in the phlegms

The rapids spit through picket-grins of moonlit mirrored trees;
Where the pour, lowering,

Draws the dark-crest-fallen tides,
(the melanchole)

Those melancholies flown down chimneyed cheeks of maountain sides,

Down the hollows,

Down to comb
the whispered washings of the feeder streams
with the pine's aeolian tone.

This long drawn lowering down the seams of ledges, growing,
whelms
in a blending, blown, and falling flow,

Minglings of slow willowed hymns

With green fountains of the elms

Below;

Draws the wind-mows and the wind-soughs of the pine-tone
Down to flow
Into minglings of slow willowed hymns

With green fountains of the elms

Below.

THE VOICE OF THE LONG RIVERS IN THE MARSHES

Light riven cries of day are all unspun.

We heard them with the rivers in the marshes fall

When,
Swinging round on widened arms,

The blue-eyed rings of lakes among the sky
vanished in chasms, plunging coldly from the sun.

Then there were heard, early in the evening air on ponds,

Demurring on the air of evening ponds,
as water jackets cooled the furnaced murk down deep,

Slower than a sigh,

The first cool fall of night,
condensing,

Closing on the bog.

The first cold breath of night descends,

Condenses on the bog,

Exhales through hoverings over humus holes below the fronds

The open hhuahhs-hhuahhs that softly heave in sleep;

Breathing lung-fish dreams of struggles

Won
dimly from auroral mists
for fire of oxygen;

Auroral mists in infant sheets,

Wrapping,
Carrying the dawn
                    down steps to us on rivers' inlets,

bibbling seeping lisps through sedged lips
of frictions feathered wetly
in the fluffed fuzz of weeds,

Mawing the glum goodbyes of sunken foliage to the sog
with foggy bubblings,
Globules going up in gasps of marsh gas,
stuttering sky-gulped gurglings through the reeds.

Then refreshed and partial roused

A voice was born upon the waters,

Winnowing orally off bars, whispering warblings slow,

Drawing the banks in gloom,
Where
Outlets tow

A wandering wind among the weeds,

A watery wind that bends the weeds,

As though it were a metronome of flow
forever wavering by.

There, where drainage swamps go down the ground,

The low-low pulse of water wash was found

To rearise in rills

Which lift the sky,

Teeming with the stream's shimmer-ringing
on light stimulated eyes in wings,
Singing,
Cheeping
In a trillion high pitched trills.

It is the helion chorus of the morn.

THE VOICE OF THE LONG RIVERS IN POWER

Out of the smouldering in the marshes of the benzene
squeezed from flags,
(Printed in the doom's-day book of sediments with chars)

Out of the hydrogen sighs of flowers, cracked with oil,
pressed flat in tomes of shale,
stuttering messages with broken lines and bars
of the black inheritance of energy and vengeance
from the dead,

Decay,

Fumes!

and accretes its catabolic climax

POWER!

Power!
leaping to the zenith of high heats and nimbus peaks,

Then plunging to the sink of cold and falls—

Trapped,

Trapped, exploding as

Boulders clamp their lime-clenched jaws on jams, dams,
rock's artillery,

Rocked artillery broadsides from the ramps,

Percussions, pops,

Percussions, spreading with the ruptured pops of pressure,
opening up,
expanding out in hops,
pouting the flood;

Puckering up the sky
in reverberations risen rumptuous from the thunder
of the plumb-dropped tonnage pounding in the pit:
Power,
pulverized to concentrate its contacts,
Reaches down the skies from stars to grip the cataract.
Creation's open, foaming fingered hand of stone
Reaches from the stars, grips the cataract,
Holds the falls, unlocks the heat in holes.
Power, smashing thru the river inner fires
With friction's incandescent gleams,
Salival and acetylene, white as a snarl,
Compressing salvos of the atmosphere
That slash thru stony teeth of spray,
Sizzling thru the fissures which they charge with spray.

Accelerations hurled the mountains backwards,
Cataracting towards the plains;
And so, on power drops,
We shot in man's canals.
Trap rock banged!
                    Mud mucked,
                                Shovel boomed,
                                            Dredge sucked—

The schist by cats and clamshell buckets clawed away.
Noon's whistles halt:
The shift,
          of man,
                of tides,
                        of sands

That hissing thru the gates,
The push's swift commands,
Stone crushed economies,
The hammer taps on T's,
Tubes—pipes—elbows,

Ribbings in the drain,
Short cuts buzzing across diagonals,
Smooth and wet with grease;
Until
That last, that final reckoning of Fate,
Black model of the cross we bore in vain,

Our Judgment Day
In flood burst coffer dams, filling with drowning men,

Where seething damps the moan,

Going like skull-split falls off trucks down flowing roads,

With gravity crashes down shafts on gravel mixers
Off cracked platforms—iron monkey wrecks
With shattered thorax, broken backs and necks,

Croaking harshly in the darkness of our towns,

Of our black marked cross—our wracked unknown—

The catastrophic climax of our Powers,

Our own—our social agony—our X!

Rolling harshly thru the darkness of our towns,

Our own—

Our social agony—our X!

INSIDE THE SNOW

The fulf of feathers in the fall of snow
Is lulled in surface areas where
It bears the hush of some numb nimbus layer
Filtering its dim thistles in the rifts of thinner layers,
Swimming under, drifting by;
Giving this fluffed undulance an edgeless semblance
Of some inner hesitance among the tumbling heavens when,
Wedding themselves still once again with their own air,
They brush the tufts of earth with pale dispersions of the sky.

Thus snow's fresh whiteness is frost's airy phase
Of lattice-scattered light among the porticos of dawn
When daylight with its tungsten flame garnishes the cornices of morn.
And this is so—whether heavied in wet weather's haze
With continuous sifted hissings in sibilance suggesting
Evidence of Heaven's lisping of its air's dimensions in its sailing lace,
Telling of pale assortments of its inner hidden presence in
The wafen crystals as if webbed wefts of icen vapors were
White parachutes of water, soft stutterers of settling-calls,
Selected echoes of wet densities; ghostly graders whispering
Of varying swiftness in the heaven's swarming falls.

And yet
when frozen-locked in solid blocks in rigid planes

Under the pounding boots, cleats, treads of Man,
his tanks, trucks, wheels,

Yet what little air is left in flakes of Heavens' breath
carries the strains

Of mechancial bruises,
and the jerked readjustments that go

Under the pressure-crushed-crunch of the heels . . .

With slippings
and the abrupt breaks of dry crystals

in the cold weather creak and the cry of the snow.

WATER

The secret in the rub and shine of water
Beneath the nimble gleams of streams and seas
Is not bright chrome's alone, nor is it mercury's.
It is the silver rust of hydrogen
Lifting high its mineral gleaming shines,
Mirrors of the hell-hot fire,
Annealed in cataclysmic drifts with oxygen:
Thus water's sheets,
White with evenly reflected light,
Steady with regular intensities,
Sparkles with the seared metallic
Features of its hydrogen, its sire.
And, thus, though spooled in cool pools
Of clustered spheres in smooth and silver innocence,
The mirrors, which the water rocks,
Are rough with frictive rips and dents,
And nicked with rust's metallic pocks.

THE NORTH WIND

When gloom of winter evening first pulls in
The North Wind goes to bed with the Old Woman.

When moans from the cedar woods begin to thin—
Oh the North Wind goes to bed with the Old Woman,
Who in her hood withdrew.

TIN RAIN

Ten tin dreams
Stem in the rain.

I try to find who knows why.

Ten tin dreams
Fill me with ten men's sighs.

When nine fly,

Then I fall low in gloom
and try to find why blind sorrows grow
from one left hovering in

Nine wet sheens

On tin.

STONY RIVER

I

Under the veil,
        Under the purl,
                Of hum-drummed waves in slow-rolled air,
Great sleep-washed monotones brought something of those long-
    spilled ways on me.
Spawned in the spell,
        Under the swirl,
Down, I slept, drifting in the incessant trickle in the flux of rivers,
On old Fahm-moods blown thru rain-lips of riffs,
Whirled from below flows cooled over water-wisped stones
On shoals of the Esopus:
River of change,
        River of fables,
                River of droned foams.

II

There, lisps in turned eddies were stone-thrown echoes of the earth's
    edges;
Churning their reverberant dirge of erosion,
Murmuring of shorn-stone, bowls, shadows, hollowed forms, storm-
    hewn urns full of low tones,
Murmuring of mowing the world's curved surface;
Its dropped creeks with its cut peaks getting calamity echoes
Sloughed, stilled, slow-towed, smoothed
By the steady, leveling ocean's pull.
There, I learned: the tare, the wear of earth's terraces
May be measured with the meadow's depth in loam.

III

Among percussions echoed thru the bones and lulled by time,
The earth's wear drew me thru, drew me down

Under distilled curtains of the ancient rains,
Under the fall,
                    the long pour,
Under mountains, slabs, tombs, monuments of slow change,
Drew me thru shadows of their faults and flaws.
There, I heard the voice of peoples on the noise of waters,
Voices borne, haunted by storms;
                    Brooding low over the storms' source;
Heard someone, old and parched, who fished the Far East's rivers,
     say:
"Thoughts on water grow all bearded."

SILK OF THE WINDS

The feather breath of love, silk of the winds, filled with sensitive
    caress—
With denizens in swift phlogiston realms
It is imbedded in a wish for wings,
Wherein the Heavens spring with kindlings of themselves.
This skip of the breath, this inner-singeing lift within us, brings:
Such nonsensical rhythms, such silly frictionless slippings in the
    winds
Such indefinite images of infinite degrees of freedom,
Yet electric with the nervous system's quick reflections
In alchemic visions of a swift transition—
Until—
The giddy circling in, the spinning in the whispered wefts
Of unstinted rhythms,
The whisking in the ether
Of exhilarants in the high-imagined tinglings in the cloves of taste,
Like the spread of ripples exploding from a shell,
Thins in peripheries of chill air
And ends nowhere.

THE VOICE OF THE BUOYS

Tightly tied as if wired to a solid bottom,
Swaying with the waves,
Repeating the beats of the deeps,
The noise of the tirelessly tossing buoys
Uncoils on, on a high widening of horizon.
The tonged recoils of the noise of the buoys,
Drawn with the long clong that iron hawsers haul
Are always calling,
Always calling,
How this rising—falling
Stays stably based upon an unchanged origin,
Beneath the sweeps.
It seems to be a lean and mineral tree
Recoiling from the buoyant whorls of salty water
In the dawns beneath the sea,
A sidewise leaning and a loil,
Whose winnowing seems unweariedly to be revealing
Blue winds keeling
Thru the interior in the sphered marine.
Yet these unwearied clongings,
When in period pealings,
These turquoise noises of the buoys
Loiter on in spite of lost spawn,
In spite of all the lost oil wasted on the bay
In spite of the mis-whifted soil seeds in the sea breeze,
In spite of Mankind's crimes, wars' wrongs,
The cries, snorts, tossed bodies of bleeding seamen
Destroyed in the deeps,
Still the buoys are always buoyant,
Always clonging on, gonging on,
Thru fogs, thru storms, warning of dangers on the way.
Pleading with their pealing,
Enjoining all who sail

To hear the toiling voice within the tongs,
Forged by peoples, nations, races from all climes;
Assayed in fire, refined and crystallized from mines,
Voicing Ahoy! Ahoy!
Alloyed chains of labor's ties!
Accouterments of time, change, song,
Silver chiming coins of continents,
Voice of Man upon the seas!

TO BOBBY

Out of breath we make you be
Luminous with unknowns
When phosphorus from our bones
Will shine upon the sea.

SECTION 2

ON ANIMALS

THE RACCOON

We saw the coon roaming in pools
To scoop with claws his moon-wink trout,
Washing Procyon in the stream;
Where only winds, besides his nimble paws,
Spread a rippling sheen.

Where feeder-streams from springs inroll,
Molten in the loud-foamed riffs, unruly in the moon,
Slower shadows of the tree limbs stroll
Along the shallows with the coon.

THE TURTLE'S SHELL

Under the turtle's shell,
Knapsack of dreams,
Atlas of the blue,
Slow mover in the streams,
Treads the tractor of a shadow
Thru the shade-world of its birth,
A penumbra of the sorrow
Of blind men stumbling in the black
Of Man trudging over the earth
Carrying cities on his back.

Under the turtle's shell,
Umbilical umbrella,
Conundrum of the thunder,
Membrane of the rain
Rolls the rock the eyes draw under,
The pill box with the peep hole
In the fortress of the shade.
Roars the blood thru armor's shadow
Under the roof that terror made,
Under brain cells scorched to stone,
In the clay burnt dome of wounds that sealed
Flesh dark memories in the bone.

Carved on the turtle's shell
Are dark lines of scars, omens of woe
For those who neither flee nor yield,
Nor strike offensively against the foe
But shrink within their skin to grow
Hardened, slowed, and cursed to be
Blinded in the shadow of their shield
Like France within her Maginot.
Hauled down dark trodden roads,

Bowed with this helmet of the dead,
Heavy as tears we cannot weep,
Here the Past, crawling thru sleep,
Bequeaths its burden like pallbearers' loads
We, the living, carry on our head.

ON THE PLAINS OF SASEBO

How frequent the nights,
sleepless,
moan-hushed,
and batted

I spent

Under the knot-gnarled arms of pines,
crying with wind strains,

By the shores of lake night-soil
on the plains of Sasebo;

Until

near a spring-fed stream east of Ishpeming
and north of Watersmeet,

where the northern lights seemed to condense
in the small ball of a silver fox,
flickering through dark spruce;

I caught a mink
in a crystal cave.

THE DIRGE OF THE COLD

Following lonely clouds of sound
On towers, tolls, bells,
Tongs of doom on darkened towns,
Following mutterings on cold stones of scuffled walks,
On crowds marching to the booms of clocks;
Harking to roars of explosions muffled in the rust and dun
Under the kinked complaints of metals on the streets,
Under the smokeless smoulderings in the junk yards and the slums,
Harking to open shouts on concrete blocks
Reporting news of wars, rumors of doom;
Disheartened with the growls of anarchic Power
Ruling all our towns:
Sorrow drove us to the northern woods.

But over the northern waters plowed with otter,
Over ponds, marshes, lacunae in cold ground,
Over the refuge from the towns only woodsmen know
Rose a floating moving sound,
The mocking call of melancholia's clowns;
The huh-hoh-hooh-hooh-hooh, huh—hoh—hooh—hooh—hooh
Of lone loons, calling hullo-oh-oh-you-oo-oo
Wanderers alone in the northern gloom,
Hunting in the cold of the northern gloom!
Hullo-oh-oh-you-oo-oo!
A tubal sound wandering far with large volume,
Starting loud but closing, falling always
With those mournful, quoovering, mooning tones
Hullo-oh-oh-you-oo-oo!
Swallowed, broken off as though some lonely human
Gulping water,
Losing bubbles thru the blue
Were drowning all alone.

Following from June to August, thru the autumn rains,
Thru November and December,
Following the dark hours, born in the storm, moving thru the gloom,
Over the frozen snow,
Floating over the farmless marshes, over the most unhuman grounds,
Homeless, roadless, huge;
Blown out of the hollows of brutes, out of their cowardly hearts,
Arose those brooding, yowling tones:
Those lonely ruthful sounds,
The open mouthed ah-ah oh-oh oo-ooo howls of coyotes and wolves,
Fathers of warning, low throated, chorded to rumble,
Nose whooing to the moon,
Nose beading the moon.
Brooding on the slowness, the low pitch, the long drawn tone
of those lonely volumes of sound
I ponder whether their slow motions are not unconscious knowledge
How out of the slowing down of all motion,
Out of the cooling down of all motions,
Grows the coldest volumes in the universe:
Where all power is lost
Among unknown zones of inscrutable gloom
Looming among the outermost stars,
Bounding an ominous darkness;
And I wonder whether those forlorn calls of the storm,
Those lonely clouds of sound,
Are not mocking our bemoaning,
Our scolding the cold, our loss of power in the cold:
Copying the slow tone of our sorrow,
Clowning our mourning over our loss of power,
On going alone to the home of ultimate cold
On the slow motion of unbounded and all-enshrouding darkness:
Whether the huh-hoh-hooh-hooh-hooh calls of the loons,
Forlorn, lonely, born in the storm,
Or the ah-oh-oh-oh oo-ooo howls of coyotes and wolves,
Or the sounds of towers, tolls, bells,
Tongs of doom upon our towns!

THE VOICE OF THE OWL

The Who Who? of the hoot owl,
The query of the dark,
The tall trees' question mark
with claws
           that cut quick nicks in bark
falls through the nightfall's cowl
on Whoo—Who he hungers to pursue.

The cruel Whoo—Whoo, cruel Who?
of the hoot owl,
                 ruthlessly unmoved,
Looks over small game's thoroughfares below,
Scrutinizing moonlit footprints on the snow,
Perusing newsprints of the woods.

Wings shielded with the wild cat's hue,
Blinkers winking in their hoods,
Evening lids which lift and droop
to cold moans of Who?—Who? . . . Who?—Who?
Who's the traveler whom he slew?
Whose bones will strew the woods?
Who? Who? Who? Whooo?

CROWS

There falls
A quarreling on,
Dark as a conqueror's shadow on
Fresh spring grain.

There's a darkness on,
A black-flapped darkness on
the jonquil sun.

That quarreling and that darkness
call a warning,

For . . . all.

It's the swartness, brashness, hook-pecked boldness
in the harsh caws of rooks,

Safely perched
on wooden shoulders of oaks,

Chattering angrily,

At their enemy,

The hawk,

Or fox.

WOOD WINDS

When in Spring
The wood winds blew in, flew in,
Putting silver in the wilderness
On the pussy willow's skin;
Bringing food to nurture winter's creatures,
Looking still so weak, so poor, so thin:
Sleepy woodchucks, bruins,
And raccoons hooking fish through windows in the streams.
We took to spearing eels—
Where the willow roots the green deeps are,
Swimming in a school of silver dreams.
When through the woods in Spring
Seedling winds blew in, flew in,
We, too, hooked in what we would need to eat;
Cooked it good, filled our innards full of dinner,
Then in sleep, like lean raccoons,
We too drink in liquid minerals, sugars with proteins,
And all the richness in the broods of living brooks
Which winter's crystal prisons bar.

SECTION 3

IN THE MIRROR OF THE NIGHTS

I

Earth broodingly withdrew

to sleep within a shadow
made out of her own body's shade

Out of whose radiations flew
a clear, but fluid name

Filled with English music in
The nights, the nights, the nights.

II

Beyond the dawn-sparks floating in the heights,

Beyond the whorls of white arms tirelessly spiraling beyond
silvery ladles and lattices of lights . . .

Huge across dark's rondure looms

The self-consuming wildness of creativity,
The cold bone in
the incandescent dice of destiny.

There it warns, like a hydrogen sigh,
through that cold die of
the hydrogen hearths in the sky . . .

and is hinting
through that cast of incandescence into stone
on spin-winking flights . . .

of more chill than the one spun
by planet dust-nets of the sun in

the noces, nuits, and nachts and nights,
and nights, and nights.

III

Above the cooling crust and gaseous envelope,
above the feathers and the dust,

The quality of islands pervades the heavens:

Assuaging the relentless, endless trend towards equilibrium
with distance,

              seeding the autonomous leavens
of the sentient and the strange rare species in the Elysium
of the uncompetitive,

              letting the singular's negation
of statistics . . . yield fulfillment thru the isolation
on lone worlds wandering in a frictionless continuum.

So ever through soft folds of curtains on dark dreams,
sewn within the veins of molten depths,

Earth extends her long, her slender cone
towards furnaces of birth and death.

And in blending strains of solitary tone,
Starting dark and open, long and slow,
then swiftly wheeling into zenith flights,

She leans
           beyond projection of her sphere

When, brooding on the shadow of herself, we hear
The nights . . . the nights . . . the nights.

Section 4

ON MUSIC

LYRIC FOR A FLUTE

The little peep, peep seeps

of a winter creek
beneath a wooden bridge,

Blowing through the wood blue-peeps,

Repeatedly reveals,

(in keeping up these drips and leaks
of little silver bibbling beads)

How aerial echoed spheres

Cooly lift balloons in beats,

Moving
        through the long, lean
sealed-in-rooms of tubes,
bowls, closed in cupolas, flues,
pipes, booths, keys, and flutes,

And the blue water bottle of the air
Between
              the lowered flow of freezing creeks

And the frozen dome each streamlet keeps
with the crystalline expansion
of its icen sheets.

With the little peep, peep, peeps,

Boobling through the winter creeks,

We hear the cool clear toots
in queer kinked tunes of flutes,
blowing
      floo-ee, floo-ee . . .

With acoustical simplicity.

Through reeds within the licker's tooth

Each Lilliputian tubal bead
leaps with a clear and silvery speed
in a series of
      floo-ees, floo-ees.
These, pursuing, plea to you and me,
(to both the old and youth)

Who will flee with me? Whoo-You?

Who will dance to these cool toots,

Who will stoop and leap in tune,

Who will, please? Whoo-You?

Whoo-He? Whoo-She? Whoo-You?

Who will go floo-ee with me?

Who will swing floo-ee with me?

Who will swing floo-ee, floo-ee,

Who-She? Who-He? Whoo-You?

Who will swoop, then kick?

Who will coast, then flit, loop and leap
in hoops and rings on peaks of toes?

Who'll be tickled with a queer-kinked tune
Those teak-timbered overtones balloon?

Who would limn their azure-looped agility
lilting with atmospheric elasticity?

To whom, to whom . . .
do these aerially blue and fluid tunes
bring boobling dreams of tone-blown beings
breathing soluble imaginings?

Who hears in these quick dimplings of the winds
a wooing whistling,
ear-wooing you to feel fluid
and free
as the flittery-moving, everywhere fluencies of air

Whose keys begin with echoed peep, peep, seeps,
beneath the ice on winter creeks

And finish with the flute's queer-kinked toots
and cool liquidities,
flittering
            woo-ees, floo-ees, woo-ees, floo-ees?

VOICES IN THE VIOLINS

With a quiet sigh of need
The sing-winds of the violins
Begin the sinuous shiverings which plead:
I, sighing, pine of need, I sigh of need.
Then a trilling on a finer, tighter line
Rises in a feline visceral whine,
With a sweet string-tingled keening,
Shrilling thin and high and fine
Until the fibres quiver with the piercing meaning
of the near hysteria which is trying to cry in
The feminine violence of the violin:
"I cry to breed, I cry to breed."

On untaut thongs then throbs a hoarseness dropping low
On the prolonged twong of long undivided strings,
Sobbing of the coarse, song-drawn, horsehair bow.

Then the violence of the violins
Rebegins to speed its vibrant highings
From the white-steamed and the kiln-dried lignins
In the seasoned cistern of the singing, rising,
With unstinted stings of female violence in the winds:
"I cry to breed, I cry to breed,
I cry to breed."

Out of the grotto, out of the polished box of varnished boards,

The mawing volume of a stronger sonance

Lobs
a long seance of qualms and chords,

That twong responses to some vast loss,
as though the rocking throbs were monologues of melancholy,
unconscious jargons of forgotten wrongs;

Twonging longings for Man's untarnished origin
on the dark tongue of some long forgotten language
on the columns of our dawn.

Then intoxicants of charm and harmonics on the thong
dissolves the long vasantas of all sorrows
in adagios of soft song,

Songs of calmness
drawing alms of solace from long thoughts,
solitary thoughts,
thoughts so sombre and so sought for,
for so long,

They fall in darkness on the carmine gardens of our organs

And wander in the haunts of concepts in the shadows
of the body's walls.

There the violins' songs grow strong, they throb! They saw!
(within those halls of mortal power, those carnal vaults)
A soft autonomous unlocking of our dawns
with warm unknottings of the bonds of thoughts;

And they VAUNT how this incarnate power,
with its promise of a sharper consciousness of sorrow

Shall assault all walls upon the morrow.

Then the high shine of the triumph, flying,

In the sing-winds and the sigh-winds

From the white pine cryings of the violins;

And the strivings of these inner-quizzing keenings

To sing a symphonizing of their meanings

Flings the whispered sweetness of the high pitched strings
into piercing quiverings which exceed in speed
the previous periods which the vibrance rings,

To rise still shriller, swifter in the sky,
(lingering with a sizy timbre in their liftings)

Until the climbing of this sinew-izing stings
its keen leaping, seizing cry:

"I cry to breed, I cry to breed."

Until these whizzings sing unceasing,

Swinging with insistent beating

of winging frequencies repeating:

"Mim—Mim—Mim, she will breed with him,

with the high pitch still increasing

in a Meem-Meem-Meem, . . .

Breed with him, breed with him,

Breed with him. . . ."

THE ORCHESTRA OF THE LANGUAGE

FINALE

If music is true
let harmony be,
If reason is real
leave peace unto me.
If number is wonder
in intangible norms,
Let percussions asunder
unite in new forms.

If creation's contagious,

let no one courageous
in face of the thunder
of our world going under,

Not seek in anarchy
the ultimate unity

Of science and symmetry.

BIBLIOGRAPHY

Aristotle. *The Poetics of Aristotle.*

Barbour, J. Murray. "Musical Sales and Their Classification." *J. Acous. Soc. Am.* 21:No. 6, November, 1949.

Black, J. W. "Natural Frequency, Duration, and Intensity of Vowels in Reading." *Journal of Speech Disorders* 14, 1949.

Castner, T. G., and C. W. Carter, Jr. "Developments in the Methods of Articulation Testing." *Bell Sys. Tech. Jour.* 12:347-370, July, 1933.

Clemenceau, George. *Rhetoric.*

Crandall, Irving B. "The Sounds of Speech." *Bell Sys. Tech. Jour.* 4:586-626, October, 1925.

Crandall, Irving B. "Dynamical Study of the Vowel Sounds." *Bell Sys. Tech. Jour.* 6:100-116, January, 1927.

Davies, A. H. *Noise.*

Dunn, H. K., and S. D. White. "Statistical Measurements of Conversational Speech." *J. Acous. Soc. Am.* 11:278-288, January, 1940.

Eisenson, J. *The Psychology of Speech.*

Fairbanks, G., A. S. House, and E. L. Stevens. "An Experimental Study of Vowel Intensities." *J. Acous. Soc. Am.*, 22:No. 4, July, 1950.

Fletcher, Harvey. *Speech and Hearing.*

Fletcher, Harvey. "Physical Characteristics of Speech and Music." Monograph. *Bell System Tech. Publ.* B-568, July, 1931.

Fletcher, Harvey. "The Pitch, Loudness, and Quality of Musical Tones." *Am. J. Physics* 14:215-223, July-August, 1946.

Fletcher, H., and R. H. Galt. "The Perception of Speech." *J. Acous. Soc. Am.* 22, March, 1950.

Fletcher, H., and J. Steinberg. "Articulation Testing Methods." *Bell Sys. Tech. Jour.* 8:806-854, May, 1929.

Hayakawa, S. I. *Language in Action.*

Hibbit, George W. *Diphthongs in American Speech.*

Ingalls, Jeremy. "Chromatic Rhyme." *Word Study* 25:1, October, 1949.

Kopp, George A., and Harriet C. Green. "Visible Speech." *J. Acous. Soc. Am.* 27, July, 1940.

Lanz, Henry. *The Physical Basis of Rime.*

Miller, Dayton Clarence. *The Science of Musical Sounds.*

Munson, W. A., and Mark B. Gardener. "Loudness Patterns." *J. Acous. Soc. Am.* 22:No. 2, March, 1950.

Ogden, C. K., and I. A. Richards. *The Meaning of Meaning.*

Paget, Sir Richard Arthur. *Human Speech.*

Parmenter, Clarence Edward, and Solomon N. Trevino. "The Lengths of the Sounds of a Middle Westerner." *Am. Speech* 9:No. 2, April, 1935.

Poe, Edgar Allan. *How I Wrote "The Raven."*

Poe, Edgar Allan. *The Philosophy of Composition.*

Poe, Edgar Allan. *The Power of Words.*

Potter, Ralph K. "Audi-visual Music." *Hollywood Quart.* 3:No. 1, Fall, 1947.

Potter, Ralph K. "Objectives of Sound Portrayal." *J. Acous. Soc. Am.* 21:No. 1, 1949.

Potter, Ralph K., George A. Kopp, and Harriet C. Green. *Visible Speech.*

Potter, R. K., and G. E. Peterson. "The Representation of Vowels and Their Movements." *J. Acous. Soc. Am.* 20:528-535, July, 1948.

Rimbeau, Arthur. *Some Poems of Arthur Rimbeau.* Lionel Abel, tr. Exiles' Press, 1939.

Sacia, C. F. "Speech Power and Energy." *Bell Sys. Tech. Jour.* 4:627-641, October, 1925.

Sacia, C. F., and C. J. Beck. "The Power of Fundamental Speech Sounds." *Bell Sys. Tech. Jour.* 5:393-403, July, 1926.

Sacia, C. F., and I. B. Crandall. "A Dynamical Study of Vowel Sounds." *Bell Sys. Tech. Jour.* 3, 1924.

Schillinger, Joseph. *The Schillinger System.*

Schlauch, Margaret. *The Gift of Tongues.*

Scripture, E. W. *Studies from Yale Psychological Laboratory.*

Snow, W. B. "Audible Frequency Ranges of Music, Speech, and Noise." Monograph. *Bell Sys. Tech. Pub.* B-591, September, 1931.

Steinberg, John C. "The Application of Sound Measuring Instruments to the Study of Phonetic Problems." *J. Acous. Soc. Am.* 6:16-24, July, 1934.

Steinberg, John C., and N. R. French. "The Portrayal of Visible Speech." *J. Acous. Soc. Am.* 17, July, 1946.

Steinberg, John C., and   French. "Factors Governing the Intelligibility of Speech Sounds." *J. Acous. Soc. Am.* 19:90, 1947.

Steinberg, J. C., and W. A. Munson. "Deviations in the Loudness Judgments of One Hundred People." *J. Acous. Soc. Am.* 8:71-80, October, 1936.

Stevens, S. S. *Hearing.*

Valery, Paul. *Variety.*

Wever, H. E. "Studies of Ocular Behavior in Music Reading." *Psych. Mono.* 55, 1943.

Index